The
ISRAEL
Canaan Dog

by Myrna Shiboleth

Alpine
Blue Ribbon Books
Loveland, CO

Library of Congress Cataloging-in-Publication Data

Shiboleth, Myrna, 1947–
    The Israel Canaan dog / by Myrna Shiboleth.
       p.   cm.
    "Second edition"—Introd.
    ISBN 0-931866-71-5
    1. Canaan dog. I. Title.
SF429.C33S48 1994
636.7'3—dc20   93-39621
                                                      CIP

This book is available at special quantity discounts for breeders and for club promotions, premiums, or educational use. Write for details.

1 2 3 4 5 6 7 8 9 0

COVER DESIGN: Bob Schram
COVER PHOTO: CCA Ch. Lahatut me Shaar Hagai, U.D. by Fallen Images
    Photography

Printed in the United States of America.

table of contents

Int. It. Ch. W.W. 1992 Lilith me Shaar Hagai.

introduction

The Israel Canaan Dog is unique among modern breeds. He is found on the borderline between all the truly domesticated and selectively-bred breeds, and the pariahs and wild dogs. The Canaan Dog has served and been closely associated with man throughout his long history, but has never been selectively bred. He owes his continued existence in a semi-wild state to his adaptability. The exigencies of nature alone determined his development along lines dictated by the principle of "the survival of the fittest"—resulting in a dog admirably suited to the harsh conditions of his natural habitat.

Having been involved with the Canaan from early in its development as a recognized breed, I have had the privilege to have known the pioneer of the breed, Professor Rudolphina Menzel. Breeding and working with "domesticated" Canaans in the land of their origin, Israel, I have also had the opportunity to observe them in the natural state, and to work with puppies and adults caught in the desert—opportunities that are becoming scarcer every day. This book is a result of many years of observing the Canaan and working with him under varied circumstances, and of breeding numerous litters. It is hoped that it will provide the public with an introduction to the true Canaan Dog.

Seven years after the publication of the first edition, we find the Canaan Dog remaining with a precarious foothold in his natural habitat, the desert of Israel. But what is important and encouraging to all of us admirers of this breed is the spread and development of the breed in many countries outside of Israel, and the growing popularity and awareness of the breed in its homeland, as a valued companion and working dog.

This second edition is intended to update the information provided in the first edition, about the breed's status at home and abroad, about achievements over the last few years, and to relate more in depth to the unique temperament and behavior characteristics of this breed which so set it apart from other dogs. New photos have also been provided of

Canaans at home and abroad that have successfully represented the breed in shows and as working dogs.

It is my hope that this edition will be of interest both to those who have become newly acquainted with the Canaan, as well as those who have been involved with the breed for years and are interested in updating their information.

Many thanks for the additional information and photos provided by club members in Israel and all over the world.

Int. It. Ch. W.W. 1991 Edom Beit Kuti, owned by Isabella Zirri (Italy).

about the author

Myrna Shiboleth was born in Chicago, Illinois, and received her B.A. from Northwestern University. On graduation, she took her first trip to Israel, where she became acquainted with the Canaan Dogs that were to become a major part of her life. After a year in Israel, she returned to the U.S. and was employed by Animal Talent Scouts of New York as an animal trainer and handler. During the next twelve months she handled a wide variety of animals: dogs, cats, camels, llamas, and a yak.

However, Myrna felt a great attraction to Israel, and the lifestyle that she had experienced during her year there. In 1969 she immigrated together with her Collie, Degel, and her first Canaan Dog bitch, Spatterdash Gimel Wafi. In Israel Myrna became acquainted with Dr. Dvora Ben Shaul and others who were interested in establishing a kennel for the purpose of breeding and preservation of the Canaan Dog. This was the start of the Shaar Hagai kennels, established in 1970, and still active and thriving today.

Over the years, more than forty Shaar Hagai dogs have completed their Israel championships, and many other International titles have been accumulated: at last count, ten International Champions, sixteen World Champions, and many other titles including obedience. Myrna presently shares Shaar Hagai Farm with her daughter, son-in-law, and a granddaughter, who already exhibits the family fascination with animals. The canine family includes Canaan Dogs, Collies, Shiba Inus, Border Collies, and Tibetan Mastiffs.

In addition to breeding and raising Canaans, Myrna has been involved in a wide variety of animal-related activities. She has owned and operated a riding stable, worked as a keeper and handler of wild animals in the Tel Aviv Safari Park, owned and managed a boarding and training kennel and worked for a number of years as a technician in animal behavior research at Tel Aviv University. She has also served as an advisor on dogs for the Israel Defense Department, and been the professional representative in Israel for Pedigree Petfoods, advising veterinarians and breeders on nutrition and behavior. From 1972-1975, she and her husband lived in Africa, where she was able to study and observe animals in the wild. As one of her projects while working at Tel Aviv University, Myrna hand-raised a hyena cub, who subsequently lived with the family as a house pet for eleven years.

Myrna has published numerous articles, in Israel and abroad, on the Canaan Dog and various aspects of dogs and their behavior. She currently is self employed as a pet behavioral therapist, runs training classes, and writes for the local dog magazines.

The author with her dog Isr. Ch. W.W. 1991 Ofra me Shaar Hagai.

history and development 1

The Canaan Dog belongs to one of the most ancient families of dogs, the Spitz family, whose members are found all over the world. The basic Spitz type has been modified over the centuries by the varied surroundings in which the dogs found themselves, and today includes a wide range of types, from the Nordic breeds of Huskies, Elk- and Bearhounds, etc., to the Basenji of Africa, and even to the Australian Dingo. However, most members of this family retain certain basic characteristics—a body build tending to be square, tail carried high and curled over the back, erect ears, a short quick trot, and personality traits of loyalty, suspiciousness of strangers and unusual things, aggressiveness, especially to other dogs, and extreme independence.

The Canaan Dog is a local development of the Spitz family in present-day Israel. It has adapted to be ideally suited to the location. A bit further north, in Syria, there are dogs of similar type, but heavier and stockier in build and with a longer coat that is more suited to the colder climate. Further to the south, the dogs of the Sinai Desert and Egypt become more slender and refined, culminating in the Pharoah Hound type. The specific type of the Canaan Dog is found only in Israel.

The breed has been known since pre-Biblical times. It is believed that Biblical references to dogs would have been to dogs of the Canaan type. Ancient drawings and carvings of dogs very close in type to the "modern" Canaan have been found—for example, in the Bene Hassan tombs (2200 - 2000 BC). The rock carvings found in Wadi Celoqua in Central Sinai show Canaan Dogs chasing an antelope (1-3rd century CE). A clear depiction of a Canaan (bas relief) has been found on a 2nd century CE sarcophagus dug up in Ashkelon.

The Canaan must always have been used as a guard dog, to protect the homes and herds of the area's residents. Occasionally he may also have served as a herding dog; there still occur Canaans with herding instincts. Through the upheavals of history he survived in this small section of the Middle East; never selectively bred, only the strongest, most

1

fit and most intelligent specimens survived the difficult conditions, developing according to the demands of their environment. They lived, for the most part, by hunting and scavenging; prime quality male pups were captured and raised by anyone requiring a guard or herd dog.

In 1934, Professor Rudolphina Menzel immigrated to Israel (then the British mandated territory of Palestine). She was already known as one of the world's foremost authorities on dogs. On her arrival, she was requested by the Haganah (Jewish Defense Forces) to build up a service dog organization. Prof. Menzel found that the breeds of dogs most commonly used for guard, tracking and war dog tasks, such as German Shepherds, Boxers, and Dobermans, suffered greatly from the difficult climate conditions, resulting in impaired efficiency. Her attention was attracted to the pariah dogs she observed in the vicinity of the Bedouin camps, Druse settlements, and in the desert and wilderness. Her observations indicated to her that this was a true native breed of dog ideally adapted to conditions in this difficult land. She named it the "Canaan Dog," after the Land of Canaan.

Observation showed that these dogs had extremely keen senses and a highly developed sense of territory and desire to guard. Determined to try them as working dogs, Prof. Menzel began a program of "redomestication." Her initial attempts were with wild and semi-wild adults living in the vicinity of her home. She began luring them with food and found that as they began to trust her, they became very devoted. She also captured litters of puppies, which she raised and found extraordinarily adaptable to domestication. She then began her own breeding program, and introduced the Canaan as a working dog. Large numbers of Canaans were provided for the Defense Forces during and after World War II. They proved to be quick, alert dogs that tenaciously protected their territory, and thrived in difficult conditions and terrain where other breeds suffered. A Canaan was one of the first dogs effectively trained to detect mines; they proved very successful in patrol and tracking work and excelled in guard work.

Rock carving from the Negev from early C.E. showing Canaan type dog chasing an ibex.

After the War of Independence (1948), Prof. Menzel became involved in a program for training seeing-eye dogs for the blind, further proving the versatility of the Canaan by training several to fill this task. She continued with her breeding and development of these dogs. Although she was never able to keep large numbers of Canaans, for reasons of space and budget, she was always interested in preserving the true wild type, and, at every opportunity, introduced new bloodlines from wild-born dogs into her breeding program.

In 1953, the Israel Kennel Club accepted the Standard of the Canaan Dog as prepared by Prof. Menzel. The breed has since been adopted as the national breed of Israel. The breed was recognized by the FCI (Federation Cynologique Internationale) in 1966, and the FCE standard was revised in 1974 and again in 1985.

Prof. Menzel's aim in breeding was to retain the original traits of the breed—their natural adaptation to climate, resistance to disease, modest requirements of nutrition and care, and unique personality. She bred numerous generations of Canaans and was instrumental in the first exports of Canaans to the US and Europe. Throughout her breeding program, she continued whenever possible to incorporate new wild stock, to retain and reinforce the basic breed characteristics and to prevent over-reliance on a small and limited gene pool.

Kaspit and Leviyah.

3

The first Canaans were exported to the United States in 1965. Professor Menzel sent four dogs, two of her own breeding and two that were wild-born. These dogs became the foundation of the breeding of the Canaan Dog in the U.S. and Canada. Over the following years, a number of additional dogs were exported, both by Menzel and by the Shaar Hagai Kennels. In addition to the U.S. and Canada, Canaans have been introduced into England, Germany, Holland, Switzerland, Finland, France, Austria, Italy, Luxembourg, Monaco, Denmark, and South Africa. Today there are active Canaan clubs in the United States, Canada, Germany, England, and Finland.

Shaar Hagai Kennels near Jerusalem, currently the major breeder of Canaans, started out in 1970 using the foundation stock consisting of dogs from Prof. Menzel's breeding and of wild-born dogs. When Prof. Menzel died at the age of 84 in May 1973, the last of her quality breeding stock, which was still being held at her kennel at the Institute for the Orientation and Mobility of the Blind outside of Haifa, was purchased by Shaar Hagai. This included the dog that became the first Israel Champion Canaan, Laish me B'nei HaBitachon (B'nei HaBitachon was Prof. Menzel's kennel suffix). He remained the chief stud dog at Shaar Hagai for a number of years, producing some outstanding offspring, and is found in the pedigree of most Israel-bred Canaans.

Today Shaar Hagai has litters that are four and five generations of their own breeding, but the policy remains to follow in Prof. Menzel's footsteps in introducing wild blood whenever possible. However, it is more and more difficult to find wild born Canaans. One of the reasons for this is the strict rabies control program in Israel, which includes the destruction of wild dog packs. Another reason is the "spread of civilization." Whereas the nomad of the desert, the Bedouin, used to keep Canaans, and one could be quite certain that his dogs were pure, he has meanwhile found it a status symbol to keep German Shepherds, Poodles, Irish Setters and the like, which have cross bred with the pure Canaans. These days, the Bedouin also travels through more populated areas with

One of the first four dogs sent to the U.S. by Prof. Menzel, Mex. Ch. Toro me Isfija. Owner: Ursula Berkowitz, Oxnard, Cal. Shown winning BOB at Ensenada, Mex., in 1968.

his herds, and his dogs have contact with "civilized" dogs that, previously, they were unlikely to have. Also, the penetration of the Defense Forces with their service dogs of various breeds into remote parts of the desert has resulted in crossbreeding.

After the Yom Kippur War (1973) there was, for a short while, an opportunity to obtain some Canaans from more remote areas. But at present it is very difficult to find pure wild Canaans. Even when one finds them, it is close to impossible to capture adults. Their instinctive suspiciousness keeps them away from traps, darts or tranquilized baits. It is sometimes possible, usually through the Bedouin, to obtain puppies.

The system of registering wild born Canaans is called the "miun" (literally - "sorting out"). To be registered in the Studbook, a dog must fulfill two requirements—he must be judged by a licensed judge of the breed as being at least "Very Good" according to the breed standard. He must then be bred to a fully pedigreed and proven Canaan, and the offspring are then judged for their apparent purity and conformity to type. Judging of wild-born dogs and of their offspring can only be done when they have attained a minimum of nine months of age.

For many years in modern Israel, Prof. Menzel's work with the Canaan was ignored by the general public, with only those who worked with the Canaan coming to appreciate him. The general public, accustomed to seeing the Canaan around the Bedouin camps, or in the fringes of settlements, called him an "Arab dog," lumping him together

Prof. Rudolphina Menzel at 80.

with the type of street dog/mongrel, often at least part Canaan, found in Arab villages and as a stray in towns. However, over the last years, there has been a tremendous change in attitude, as the demand for an effective and easy to manage and care for home guard dog increased. The Canaan has become highly appreciated for his qualities of territoriality, devotion, alertness and tenacity in guarding, and is greatly in demand as a home guard dog. They are also the preferred guard dogs of the Isreal Defense Forces (IDF) and are often used for patrol work. There is also increasing interest in the Canaan abroad.

Most modern domestic breeds have been selectively bred for generations to conform to certain characteristics of temperament and appearance required to fulfill the tasks for which that breed was developed. In the last generations, the emphasis has been much more on appearance, especially as relating to the show ring. There are hardly any domestic, recognized breeds that have remained, as the Canaan, completely natural, unchanged by human intervention, and an example of nature's law of "survival of the fittest." It is our hope that, although he is now being selectively bred, breeders will keep in mind what the Canaan Dog is, and will take care that he remains a natural dog, with his distinctive characteristics.

Sufa me Petra, a red gold bitch brought over as a tiny puppy from the Red Rock in Jordan by the Bedouin. A show winner and top producer. One of the foundation dams of Shaar Hagai Kennels.

A beautiful type Canaan in the desert near Arad.

Terramara's Achad Int., Mex., CCA Ch. Top dog of the year at the Tournament of Champions, Detroit 1988. Bred and owned by Terry Bagley (Canada).

Int. It. Ch. W.W. 1992 Lilith me Shaar Hagai. (Int. Isr. Ch. W.W. Sirpad me Shaar Hagai ex Gali me Shaar Hagai.) Owned by Isabella Zirri (Italy).

observations
in nature   2

by Dr. Dvora Ben Shaul

The Dog of Canaan, first described by the late cynologists Dr. Rudolf and Prof. Rudolphina Menzel, is an excellent subject for study as the animals exist in Israel today in three separate states; the Pariah or free-living state, the semi-domesticated state as exemplified by those following the Bedouin encampments, and the truly domesticated Canaan dog in the homes and kennels of dog fanciers. For the purposes of this study the animals are referred to as "free-living," "bedouin," or "domestic" according to the following criteria:

"Free-living Canaan Dogs" - These Canaans are usually found in the semi-wastelands of the Judean hills, the Galilee, the Negev and the southern Aravah. The source of these free-living packs is obscure but it is clear that the line between them and the semi-domesticated Canaan dog of the Bedouin tribe or the Arab village is a thin line indeed, for in the wake of the Six Day War in 1967 when the Golan area was evacuated by the Syrians, those village-bred Canaan dogs that managed to survive the eradication procedures of the Rabies Control Service reverted within a matter of months to truly feral packs roaming the hills and knowing no master. These packs exist today and have in a few years lost all traces of the former domestic habits of their forebears. The free-living pack is self-contained, suspicious of all humans and highly territorial toward other animals, particularly wolves, jackals and hyenas. It is usually composed of 5 to 15 members. The pack sustains itself by hunting hares, partridge, mice and voles but does not disdain refuse dumps or any other food source available, and occasionally turns marauder of sheep and calves. One must here include those female Canaan dogs that have a loose attachment to the movements of a particular Bedouin encampment. The Bedouin rarely if ever feed these bitches and their attachment to the encampment seems to be based on the affinity of a bitch for a particular Canaan Dog domesticated by the Bedouin. The bitch lives more often than not by her wits and cunning, hunting and foraging in the scant refuse of the camp and stealing when the opportunity arises. The Bedouin tolerate her as source of male pups to be impressed into service as guards for the encampment. Rarely is a bitch kept by the Bedouin and the classic statement of the Bedouin on the matter is "El Kelbe min Allah" (The bitch belongs to God). One can only consider these bitches as feral animals living in proximity to the Bedouin camp.

There is good reason to suspect that the free-living pack may represent a family or clan unit. This is supported particularly by pack color patterns. The sand colors are recessive to black while the spotted pattern is recessive to solid patterns, and it is interesting to note that when a pack is predominantly composed of sand-colored individuals then no black and white members ever appear. The same is true for solid pattern—a pack wherein most members are black and white will occasionally produce sand-colored members, with the same being true for spots; this is compatible with the genetics of a family pack.

"Bedouin Canaan Dogs" - These dogs are practically always only one step removed from the free-living Canaan. They are in most cases taken as pups from the den of a free-living bitch and are tied up in the encampment until mature. They are fed and maintained by the Bedouin due to their value as camp guard dogs, particularly guarding the flocks against wolves, hyenas and feral dog packs. These dogs, at first impression, appear to be extremely cowardly but, in truth, are highly suspicious, for in the day to day life of the camp, the approach of a human may mean the tossing of a piece of bread, the flinging of a stone or a kick in the ribs if proximity allows. The semi-domesticated Bedouin Canaan is ready for what comes, thence his suspicious and "fight-flight" posture at all times. Conditioned to maltreatment, the Bedouin Canaan is wary of humans and alerts the camp to any and all strangers approaching; this is to the liking of the very xenophobic Bedouin and usually earns a reward, either in the positive sense of a flung scrap or the negative sense of at least not being punished. Thus the Bedouin Canaan dog learns his duty. Faced with animal marauders, however, the Canaan is fearless, for here the all important matter of territorial prerogative is involved. In most cases the Bedouin are unable to catch or touch these semi-domesticated dogs and even when faced with an irate rabies control officer who issues an ultimatum of "catch him for vaccination or I must shoot him" are unable to secure the dog. In these cases only the children of the encampment are at times able to help, for the dogs seem to trust them and approach them freely. The Bedouin Canaan is with, but not of, the encampment and while rarely straying is not in any sense either a pet or a possession.

"Domestic Canaan Dogs" - These dogs are those maintained as household pets, security dogs kept by the military or police, and kennel stock at the Shaar Hagai Kennel near Jerusalem, devoted to the perpetua-

10

A puppy being raised in the camp. He has been captured from a wild mother and is kept tied until old enough to go out with the herds.

Bedouin dog at rest, but still suspicious - note the ear position.

Reshef me Naot Hamidbar, one of the very few Canaans brought in from the wild as an adult.

11

tion of the breed. Most of these dogs are registered in the Stud book of the Israel Kennel Club and though the majority are of domestic breeding, many were registered by selection from Bedouin stock or free-living dogs. For most of the "selected" dogs there are good bases of information on their origins. Another group is the American-bred Canaan Dogs originally of Israel stock. There are over 500 such dogs in the USA. The only other source of domestic Canaans is the Arab villages where the Canaan dogs are more domesticated than in the Bedouin encampment. Both bitches and males are kept, pups are born within the periphery of the settlement and all are more or less fed and kept by the villagers. Unlike the Bedouin Canaan, the village Canaan can be caught or handled by his master and though extremely wary of strangers is in most cases a domestic dog, albeit not well kept.

The free-living pack

There is as yet insufficient information as regards the exact social structure of the free-living pack but enough observations have been made to rule out the theory of absolute male dominance. The packs observed have ranged from five or six dogs to as many as twenty and in all cases have been of mixed sexes with some pups of less than a year forming a part of the pack, although pups of less than seven or eight months have never been observed in the pack itself, being more often seen with a

Dugmona, called Nana, one of Prof. Menzel's last and best known brood bitches. Wild born.

solitary bitch or in some cases a pair, male and female, ranging in the same general area as the pack but not with the pack itself. Although severe fighting has been observed on occasion between two or more males, or between two bitches, there have also been observations of serious fights between a bitch and a dog and in some cases the bitch was the winning contender. These fights, usually spontaneous, appeared in most cases to be over food or territorial invasion in the feeding area. Near Quneitra the author observed seven Canaans, four dogs and three bitches, feeding on the carcass of a dead cow. During the first three hours of the evening from seven to ten p.m., the feeding Canaan pack threatened and routed several foxes and two other dog packs. In one encounter a large bitch of the original pack fought for some four minutes in a slashing, bitter battle with a male from the invading pack somewhat larger than she. At last he slank away, his chest and face covered with blood. After this encounter the invading pack waited about half a kilometer from the carcass and only when the original pack had finished feeding and wandered off did they approach. The male that had fought with the bitch was seen to be limping and ate very little.

Within the pack itself fighting occurs over food when one member gets too close to another while feeding, and over bitches in estrus, but there is far less of this sort of fighting than one would suppose for reasons that will be discussed later.

The pack is principally nocturnal in its migrations and feeds in the first three or four hours after twilight and again at dawn. Though these

Cheda me Har Hazeitim - "Enigma from the Mt. of Olives," wild born bitch.

are the principal feeding hours, observations have been made of feeding at almost all other times of day but these feedings were chance encounters with food while the twilight and dawn feedings were deliberate searches for food in accustomed places such as refuse pits.

Marauding around calving pens, piggeries, sheep folds and fowl runs is always in the early evening or the dawn hours. Fowl including large turkeys are carried off to another place to be eaten while larger animals such as calves are consumed on the spot. The calf is usually brought down by biting the flanks and the neck. Piglets and lambs are usually carried away. The pack will take advantage of poor fencing or runs in disrepair but have also been known to dig under fences and enlarge small fence breaks in order to gain access to food. On one occasion in the upper Negev, a single male Canaan was observed by the author as he chased down and killed a fully adult male gazelle and fed on the carcass.

Although the feral pack forms an eternal target for the Rabies Control Service, the control officers admit to limited success, as the Canaan Dog is poison-shy, trap-wise and harder to hunt with a rifle than most truly wild animals. Most officers report that having once fired on a member of a pack from a jeep, the entire pack then seems to recognize the sound of the motor of that particular vehicle. Traps are useless except for the very large wolf traps and even these are often identified by the dogs as traps. The Canaan pack is no less adept than the wolf at detecting the presence of man-made designs against his kind. Many investigators feel certain that the wolf, *Canis lupus pallipes*, may be the ancestor of the local pariah dogs and if this be the case the changes brought about by evolutionary processes did little to change their ability to avoid danger. For this reason, despite all efforts on the part of farmers and Rabies Control officers, the feral packs still exist in almost every area suitable to their needs. Feral packs in the last thirty years have become extremely adept at utilizing the "no man's land" along the cease-fire lines and the military maneuver areas as permanent bases for rest during the day, being relatively secure except when troops are on maneuver, whereupon they move off for a time. The areas along the cease-fire lines, where human interference is at a minimum, have also become a choice denning site for bitches with pups.

Not much is known about the structure or formation of the feral pack but it is certain that on occasion semi-domesticated village Canaans do join up on a permanent or temporary basis with a free-living pack in the area. On the other hand, occasional members of a free-living pack may opt for a semi-domestic life in the proximity of a village. This often happens when a member of a free-living pack is injured or otherwise unfit for pack life.

Pregnant bitches near to whelping and nursing bitches are often seen feeding with the pack, but appear to leave the pack at other times and have not been observed with young pups in the pack. Some nursing bitches appear to remain separate from the pack throughout the period of maternal care which seems to extend through the first six or seven months and are seen accompanied by their half-grown pups as a small pack. Some observations have shown the presence of both a bitch and a dog with the pups.

Pups are usually whelped in a den dug by the bitch in a hillside. The den most often is more or less L-shaped, going in and then turning left where a rounded hollow is created. The pups are usually in the rounded inner den but appear to crawl into the wider portion to be nursed. One semi-feral bitch, taken with her two-week-old pups near a Bedouin enclave was placed in an earthen-floored kennel enclosure where the bitch immediately dug a den almost exactly like the one in the Negev where she had whelped, this despite the fact that the original den was in soft loess while the latter was in terra rosa, two soils of completely different consistencies. These pups were observed at two and one half weeks to crawl out of the den to evacuate their bowels and then return to the den. Their evacuations were then eaten by the bitch. At no time has a den been found to be soiled with any form of food or excrement.

Water is a commodity to be cherished throughout most of Israel, and free-living packs must have a water source. Usually the source is a spring or seepage in the area, but on occasion the dogs utilize puddles in irrigated land and have been known to bite into polyethylene irrigation pipes to get water. When large puddles exist in fields or orchards, the dogs often roll themselves in the soft mud and allow it to dry on their pelts, shaking it off when dry. In general, the pelt is clean and examination of a large number of free-living Canaans shot by Rabies Control officers showed that the dogs carry few ectoparasites. Ticks, the bane of many wild animals and domestic dogs, are few and usually only behind the ears and at the back of the neck. In all other areas of the body the dogs have been observed to pull off the ticks with their teeth and eat them. Bitches have been observed both in the feral state and in kennels performing this service for their pups even when the pups were half a year old and as large as their dam. The reason for fewer fleas than one would expect is not known but it is possible that the extremely thick undercoat is unattractive to these parasites.

Bedouin Dog.

Isr. Ch. Lapid me Shaar Hagai.

the breed

standard   3

The standard of the Canaan Dog is intended to describe a sturdy, agile and adaptable desert dog, totally suited to survival in the difficult climate and terrain of his native land.

Professor Menzel described two recognizable types of Canaan, and both were allowed according to the original standard that she prepared in the 1950's. These were referred to by her as the "collie type" — referring not to the collie that we know from the Lassie films, but to the Border Collie; she discerned great similarities in skull shape between Canaan and Border Collie — and the "dingo type," considered by her a more primitive and less developed form of the breed. The two types were still recognized by the Federation Cynologique Internationale (FCI) in the standard adopted in November 1966, but in later revisions of the standard, in September 1974 and the currently accepted standard of November 1985, the dingo type, by agreement between the Israel Kennel Club and the FCI, was eliminated.

The dingo type was considered "one step down" on the evolutionary ladder from the collie type; Menzel felt that it was one of the stages in the development of the breed, which resulted in the collie type as the final product. Thus the collie type, being the "final" result of evolution, is considered the ideal.

The dingo type is described in the standard of 1966 in terms of its difference from the collie type. These involve a body shape tending to the rectangular rather than square as desired, a shorter and less elegant neck, drop or semi-drop ears (what is often called a "button ear" — a small rounded drop ear, not a large, houndy ear), a heavier and more massive head with a pronounced stop and shorter muzzle. As the standard stated, "The head appears to be the original gross shape of the collielike, ennobled head shape, as generally the whole dingolike type appears to be the heavier original form of the collielike Canaan Dog." The dingo type can still be seen with the Bedouins in some areas today.

The FCI Standard (Revised 1985)

> **General Appearance:** *A medium sized, well balanced, strong and square dog resembling the wild dog type. Strong distinction between the sexes.*
> **Weight and Size:** *Height 50–60 cm., males generally considerably larger than females. Weight 18–25 kg.*

What is the "wild dog type" that the Canaan is meant to resemble? The Canaan belongs to a group of dogs known as "pariah dogs," a large and widely distributed group of half-wild or feral dogs found across southern Asia and Europe as well as northern and eastern Africa, and which also includes the dingo of Australia. In behavior, it has been found that these dogs may occupy the full range between absolute wildness and full domestication. Furthermore, any animal, regardless of its place at birth within this range, can adapt itself to a changing environment, either towards wildness or domestication. Professor Menzel and Shaar Hagai Kennels tamed a number of wild pariahs which later could not be distinguished in behavior from those born to domestication; conversely, instances are known of dogs returning to the wild and doing very well there. Many of the pariah dogs, like the Canaan, are to be classified in the Spitz family of dogs.

Despite their immense geographical range, pariahs and dingolike dogs show considerable similarity. They are animals of medium size, mostly very powerful for their size, often tawny or reddish although some are black or spotted. The coat is usually of medium length, harsh and thick. Pariahs commonly have prick ears that turn obliquely outward rather than stand perfectly straight.

Dina me Daron, a wild born bitch of outstanding type and temperament, an extremely influential brood bitch both for Prof. Menzel, and later for Shaar Hagai Kennels. A great number of Canaans still trace back to her.

Within this general description, several types occur according to geographical regions. In the Middle East alone, there is a range from the heavy, very thickly coated Syrian herding dogs, through the medium built, medium to short-coated Canaan, more refined in build and head shape, to some extremely refined types found in Egypt and Sinai, seeming to hold a halfway position between the Canaan and the desert sight hounds. Even further south, we see the small and extremely refined and short coated Basenji, but still a primitive breed with many common characteristics.

Pariahs have been known for thousands of years and were thought of as mongrels — once-domestic dogs and their descendents that had taken to the wild. Currently, scientific opinion tends to think that they represent an original strain of wild dog which has not yet become fully domesticated. The constant characteristics which have maintained themselves over millenia argue against these animals simply being mongrels fleeing civilization. They seem to have been wild animals which achieved and maintained a semidomesticated, more or less symbiotic relationship with man. Certainly as far as the Canaan is concerned this appears to be true. The Canaan is no man's slave, but rather his partner, and he reserves the right to choose the terms of that relationship.

The Canaan is a medium sized dog, rather elegant in build in relation to his size. He should never be a heavy or massive animal, but neither should he be overly fine in bone. He must always give an impression of strength, balance and capability. The comparative lightness is an adaptation to his way of life — a smaller, lighter animal requires less food and water, is more agile in escaping danger, and can find hiding places more easily. As a rule, desert animals tend to be smaller than forest animals.

However, I find it necessary to warn against a tendency I see towards creating a "mini-Canaan." The Canaan in nature and in his work as a Bedouin herd guard has to be capable of standing up to jackals, hyenas and wolves — and this does mean standing up to them to protect his flock, not running away. He has also proven himself capable of hunting and taking down an adult gazelle. Fine boned animals weighing about 12 to 15 kg.(26 to 33 lbs.) and standing well under the 50 cm. (19.5 inch) minimum height stated in the standard are totally incorrect and undesirable, and incapable of filling the purposes of the breed, as much so as oversized and massive animals.

The dingo type, much heavier in build and bone and close to the type of the heavy pariah and herding dogs of Syria and Turkey, is less well adapted to desert life. It is, therefore, not surprising that this type is not usually found in the desert but ranges more often in the rocky north of the country or in the vicinity of settlements or Bedouin camps where the chances of survival by scavenging are better.

There are a number of environmental (as opposed to genetic) reasons for the male often being much larger than the female. The female Canaan in the wild frequently doesn't achieve her full growth due to lack of sufficient food and the demands on her, perhaps, of an early litter of puppies. Males, by contrast, only have to provide for themselves. Males captured by Bedouins as young puppies and raised in camp were always selected from the largest and strongest pups in the litter. Never lacking in food, they always grew to be much larger than the wild bitches in the vicinity and were usually larger than the wild males as well. On the rare occasions that we saw bitches kept by the Bedouin, they were not very much smaller than the males, and were usually larger than the average wild bitch.

Now, after some generations of planned breeding and "domestication," we find much less difference in size between males and females. There is always, however, a very clear distinction between dog and bitch — the dog must look strong and masculine, and even a large, well boned bitch must look feminine. It should be possible, even from a distance, to distinguish a dog from a bitch.

> **Head:** *Well proportioned, blunt wedge shape of medium length, appearing broader due to low set ears. Skull somewhat flattened. Some width allowed in powerful male heads. Stop shallow but defined. Muzzle sturdy, of moderate length and breadth. Jaws should be strong. Lips tight. Nose black.*

The primary reason for the modern Canaan being referred to as "collie-type" is due to the great similarity in skull shape between the Canaan and the early type of collie, a skull shape still common in today's Border Collie.

From the front, the Canaan's head is a perfect wedge, fairly broad between the ears, tapering evenly down to the full muzzle. There should be no flaring at the cheeks or narrowing at the muzzle; the tapering should be continuous. There should be no appearance of elongation. The standard does not call for an elongated wedge, but a blunt, medium length wedge shape. One of the most common head faults is the overly elongated appearance, to the point of resembling a sighthound head, caused by too much length, too little space between the ears, or ears that are too closely set.

From the side, the head should appear to consist of two fairly parallel lines of the skull and top line of the muzzle, divided by an obvious but not exaggerated stop. The topline of the skull is not totally flat, but slightly rounded. The line of the underjaw is approximately parallel to the top line of the muzzle. The jaws should be full and powerful, never receding or weak.

The head must always be in proportion, and should never appear heavy or overly fine; however, there is a distinct difference between a strong masculine head, which will be powerful, and a typical bitch's head, which must be more feminine and refined, though never lacking in strength.

Although only the black pigmented nose is allowed by the standard, and is the only reasonable color for a desert animal that may be exposed to many hours of strong sunlight, there is a factor in the breed for what is called the "snow nose." The nose leather of the snow-nosed dog may vary in color at various times of the year and, depending on how much the dog is out in the sun, may change from pinkish to totally black. The "snow nose" will be black when the dog is out in the sun, thus providing him with adequate protection from harm from the sun's rays. There is also a liver nose, associated with the liver colored coat. This nose never turns black, and is prone to be affected by the sun; this color is not suited to a desert animal and is undesirable. The highest preference is given to the permanently black nose.

Ears: *Erect, relatively short and broad, slightly rounded at the tip and set low.*

The Canaan's ears must be prick, as are the ears of all the wild canines. The prick ear is an adaptive device for survival; the flap of the erect or prick ear serves as a backdrop for catching the sound, while its mobility helps to pinpoint the direction from which the sound came. As in most of the pariah dogs, the Canaan's ears are not erect and pointed, like the German Shepherd's ears, but stand outward obliquely and are rounded slightly at the tips.

The so called "collie-tipped" ear, a semi-prick ear that is one of the most common ear faults, seems to be an incomplete expression of the gene for the pricked ear. Drop ears or "button" ears, most often found in the dingo type or in mixes of the two types of Canaan, are completely undesirable, and should also not be used for breeding. This seems to be a recessive gene, and using them for breeding will just continue to perpetuate this fault.

Eyes: *Dark brown, slightly slanted, almond shaped. Dark rims essential.*

The unique expression of the Canaan is one of his most appealing features, and a great part of this correct expression is dependent on the eye shape and color. Improperly shaped or set eyes, or eyes that are too light in color, can completely spoil this expression, giving the dog a hard or aggressive appearance. The ideal eye is very dark, even almost black, almond shaped, set slightly obliquely, and outlined with black "eyeliner," creating a melting, Oriental, "sloe eyed" look. Pale and liver eye rims greatly detract from this expression, as do eyes that are light in color. Yellow eyes do occur occasionally and are totally undesirable; this eye color is often associated with undesirable coat colors as well. Lighter shades of brown or hazel do occur fairly frequently in the red and light brown colored dogs, and although technically acceptable if not lighter than the coat color of the dog, these colors do tend to cause a rather hard and threatening expression which is foreign to the breed. Too large or round eyes create a rather "stupid" or staring look, and eyes that are too small or piggy result in a "mean" expression. Very dark and well shaped eyes should always be highly preferred.

Mouth: *Full dentition with scissors or plier bite.*

The plier bite (level bite), which was the preferred bite in the original standards of the breed, is also commonly found in wolves, jackals, and foxes. This is an effective bite for an animal that must groom itself, pull thorns and stickers from its coat, and remove parasites such as fleas and ticks. These activities are more difficult with the scissor bite which is common to most breeds. Some cynologists say that the scissor bite was artificially created through selective breeding. At any rate, it is becoming more and more common in the Canaan and is entirely acceptable. However, under no circumstances should the original, level bite be penalized.

A study done by Dr. Dvora Ben Shaul concluded that dental faults such as defective bite and missing teeth are not unknown in a variety of breeds. In general we attribute these faults to errors of breeding in long-domesticated breeds. The observation of these faults in free-living packs of Canaan Dogs and in Bedouin bred animals is therefore of interest.

Shimshon me Shaar Hagai (Nadav me Shaar Hagai ex Bat Hol me Shaar Hagai). An excellent type, and a most influential sire.

Wide scale destruction of dogs for the purpose of rabies control in the Israeli occupied areas of the Syrian Heights for some months after the Yom Kippur War provided an interesting opportunity to survey the state of dentition in Canaan Dogs in this area. Eighty-six dogs that had been killed by rabies control services were chosen as representative of the Canaan breed standard. Fifty-four males and thirty-two females were chosen; all were adult as judged by dental development. Results of examination were as follows:

Type of bite: Scissor: 33   Level (plier): 53
Faulty bite: Overshot: 3   Undershot: 0   Uneven arrangement: 2
Missing teeth: Missing first premolar: 19
              Missing second premolar: 3
              Other teeth missing: 0
Total dogs with missing premolars: 22

The fact that at least one-fourth of dogs examined were lacking one premolar is not too surprising if one takes into account the fact that the semi-wild, free-living Canaan is in fact a highly inbred animal as the prevalence of specific color patterns within the pack would indicate. One must conclude therefore that genes for faulty dentition are widely present in even half-domesticated canine stock and are easily brought into prominence by inbreeding.

While faulty bite may well carry a penalty and a selection may be made in favor of a level bite, it is doubtful if the presence or absence of a premolar exercises any real control over the condition of the dog and therefore does not seem to be controlled in the pack by any form of natural selection.

We have also found that the Canaans seem to have a tendency to wear down or lose first premolars from about five years of age, although they do not tend to lose teeth in general, and their teeth do not deteriorate even at a very advanced age. We have seen adults of twelve to sixteen years with teeth in excellent condition and full in number.

Neck: *Muscular, of medium length.*
Body: *Square, withers well developed, back level, loins muscular, chest deep and of moderate breadth, ribs well sprung. Belly well tucked up. Moderate angulation. Balance is essential.*
Forequarters: *The shoulders should be oblique and muscular, elbows close to the body. Forelegs perfectly straight.*
Hindquarters: *Powerful, well bent stifles. Hocks well let down. Strong buttocks, lightly feathered.*
Feet: *Strong, round and catlike with hard pads.*

The Canaan is a square dog, like many of the related Spitz breeds. He is not a massive dog, but well proportioned and with medium bone. He has a very deep, though not overly broad chest, giving plenty of lung and heart space. The Canaan should never be overly heavy as this trait would be an anti-survival factor in his natural desert environment: food requirements to support a heavy body would be exorbitant, and the corresponding lack of agility would result in difficulties catching his natural prey, for the most part small animals such as rodents. However, the Canaan should also never be too light or fine in build and should not tend to the wind-hound type. He should always give the impression of solidity, compactness, strength and agility. A rangy or leggy appearance would definitely be considered faulty, as would fine bone.

The tuck up is quite pronounced, especially in young dogs. A young dog may appear rather leggy and lacking in substance. It is important to take into consideration that the Canaan is a slow maturing breed which doesn't finish maturing and filling out until three to four years of age. We find that our dogs start looking their best and just coming into their prime at four to five years of age.

The neck should be long enough to give a well-balanced, elegant appearance to the dog, but again should not tend to the wind-hound type. The neck should be very muscular.

Ch. Lapid me Shaar Hagai - a nice strong masculine head.

Head study of Ch. Laish me Bnei HaBitachon, marvelous expression and perfect ear set.

The square build and moderate angulation result in the correct balance and gait. An elongated body will result in an elongated loping stride or choppy movement, and often results in a soft topline as well. Incorrect angulation will also result in incorrect gait. Overangulation, while appearing attractive and "flashy" in a standing dog, will result in lack of agility and over-reaching in movement. The correctly built Canaan will not resort to the "fatigue gait" of pacing.

Particular stress must be laid on the difference between the Canaan and the German Shepherd. The Canaan is square with short loins and moderate angulation. He has a slender neck and a short trot. The Shepherd is elongated with extreme angulation, a sloping topline and a thick neck, and has a long, loping stride.

Tail: *Set high, thick brush carried curled over the back.*

Correct tail carriage is indicative both of correct structure and of character. The correctly carried tail is carried curled over the back and should come past the line of the back; in some cases the tail even forms close to a double curl. Although the double curl is not ideal, it is preferable to a loose tail that doesn't reach the back line and is carried like that of a Siberian Husky.

Ofri me Shaar Hagai - excellent profile.

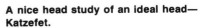

A nice head study of an ideal head— Katzefet.

In many cases, the incorrect tail carriage is caused by the tail being too low set. The base of the tail should be set high on the croup with no dip from the backline to the tail. A low set tail is often connected with an overly long back or overangulated hindquarters, the result being apparent also in the dog's gait. Be aware that the tail is not merely an appendage set on as an afterthought. It is an integral part of the dog's body construction and an incorrect tail indicates other structural faults as well.

The dog who carries his tail down consistently is insecure and fearful — these points should definitely be considered when judging the dog. Although the Canaan does not have to carry his tail high at all times, when moving in the ring his tail should be curled over his back.

Coat: *Outer coat dense, harsh and straight, of short to medium length. Undercoat close and profuse.*

The correct coat type is the short to medium harsh outer coat, similar in texture to that of many of the Spitz breeds, with a very dense and woolly undercoat. During the hottest times of the year the undercoat is shed out, leaving a harsh and strong outer coat, somewhat standoff, which provides insulation and protection from the sun. It should be noted that in hot climates the dogs that suffer the most from the heat and sun are *not* those breeds with thick or long coats, but those with very short, flat coats and no undercoats, such as Pinschers or Boxers.

During the shedding season, the Canaan sheds out tremendous quantities of undercoat, shedding in patches like wolves and jackals, usually starting at the hind quarters and progressing forward and upward.

The correct texture of the coat is coarse, not silky. There is a long coat factor in the breed; however, that is usually quite long, silky and soft in texture, and does not provide good protection against harsh weather conditions. This type of coat is totally undesirable.

It may be asked why a dog coming from a hot climate such as Israel needs a weatherproof coat. The answer is that the desert climate is very severe and has a wide range of conditions. Nights in the desert are often bitterly cold, especially in winter, while days are extremely hot. There is not a great deal of rainfall, but there can be sudden and very heavy rains which may even continue for several days, causing flash floods. There is occasionally even snowfall. Correct coat is essential to survival of the dog; an incorrect coat or lack of undercoat are very serious faults.

The thick mane found in males, and in many females as well, serves to protect the dog's neck from attack by other animals.

Color: *Sand to red-brown, white, black, or spotted, with or without mask. If masked, mask must be symmetrical. Black mask permitted on all colors. White markings are permitted* *on all colors; "Boston terrier" patterns are common. Grey, brindle, black-and-tan, or tricolor are unacceptable. Desert colors — sand, gold, red, cream — are most typical of the breed.*

Color seems to be initially related to the area from which the dog originated. Black and black-and-white Canaans were most frequent in the rocky and wooded north of the country, while the dogs seemed to become lighter in color the further south into the desert one went. Most of Professor Menzel's original stock came from the Druze villages and from free-living packs in the area in which she lived north of Haifa; thus many of her original dogs and a large percentage of the dogs from her breeding were black-and-white. The solid colors are the most common in the desert. It is rare to find blacks there, as black is not suited to desert areas due to its heat-absorbing qualities. It also stands out in areas where the natural coloration is various shades of red and sand colors. Neither is solid white common, although it does exist and is a permitted color. It also tends to stand out too visibly from its surroundings. The most common colors in the desert are shades of sand, red, gold, and brown, with or without white markings.

Left to right: Mex. Ch. Chia of Gray Mesa, World and Mex. Ch. Amos of Grey Mesa, Mex. Ch. Hora of Shaar Hagai (Dam of the other three in photo), Int. Mex. Ch. Joshua of Grey Mesa. (Sire of this litter is Spatterdash Yawvin)

One interesting point is that we have met several Bedouin who on purpose keep a black or black and white dog with their others, the idea being that the group of dogs is then visible and identifiable at greater distances. The other colors of the Canaan tend to blend in so well with the landscape that it is very hard to see them, even from quite close up.

Although the mask pattern appears to be quite random, the symmetrical mask is preferred for its attractiveness. It is not uncommon for puppies to be born with partial or asymmetrical masks, and these are not considered show quality. However, we would not penalize (either in or out of the show ring) an excellent dog for a mask that did not completely cover its ears.

There are a number of the Spitz breeds, including Siberian Huskies, Akitas, Shibas, Malamutes, and others, where the reverse mask is common — that is, a mask that is lighter in color than the body color. This is also quite common in the Canaan and is perfectly acceptable.

Grey is a naturally occurring color in the Canaan, sometimes a solid pewter grey and sometimes grey shadings on an other-colored dog. It is quite common for cream-colored adults to be born grey. There is a great deal of color change in the Canaan from birth to adulthood; the adults of some of the most beautiful golden and red shades are usually born a muddy brown, often with a good deal of black shading, which

Right: Eytan me Shaar Hagai - perfect eye shape and placement, ideal expression.

Below: Di-Zahav me Shaar Hagai (Ch. Ophir Beit Elron ex Dina me Shaar Hagai) moving out at a quick trot.

28

fades away as the puppies grow. True grey, however, is undesirable, as is the mixture of black, white, and sometimes brown hairs in the coat that gives a grey impression from a distance.

Tricolor, which refers to the true black, brown and white pattern as in a beagle (not "shaded brown," where brown areas may be shaded with some black, usually at the edges) does not seem to be a true Canaan color and when found may indicate mixed blood. The same is true of brindle. Menzel objected to the inclusion of these colors and of black-and-tan as lacking distinction and being too similar to the colors of common European breeds.

Black-and-tan is apparently a definite genetic factor in the breed and has appeared in the offspring of parents of all colors. In most instances where two light colored parents produced an apparently black or black-and-white puppy, this proved in fact to be a case of the black-and-tan factor.

Liver color is definitely not acceptable by the FCI standard. We have never in Israel seen a naturally occurring liver Canaan, and feel that this factor also may be indicative of introduction of foreign blood at some point. From what we have seen, some of the liver dogs also appear to have very short and flat coats, which are not typical to the breed.

Vatik BaAretz me Shaar Hagai (Ch. Laish me Bnei HaBitachon ex Dina me Darom), a marvelous young dog, unfortunately killed in an accident at a year of age.

Connected with this color is the factor for liver or self colored nose and eye rims, and in most cases hazel to yellow eyes. The light eye is definitely highly undesirable.

Color inheritance in the Canaan is quite complex, involving many factors including the various pattern factors. Although there are many color variations and shadings, what appears to be true is that the black is dominant to light colors, and the solid or solid pattern is dominant to spotted. The exact inheritance pattern of the various shades is not clear. For example, true rich red seems to be an extremely difficult color to breed. There also seems to be a crypto-black factor, where a white or cream dog, always with excellent dark pigmented eyes and nose, when bred to another light Canaan, will produce black puppies as well as light ones. This appears to be a case of a genetically black dog appearing light. We have had a number of dogs with this factor, including Int. Ch. Sirpad me Shaar Hagai.

Gait: *Quick, light and energetic trot. Should demonstrate marked agility and stamina. Correct movement is essential.*

The correct gait of the Canaan is one of the factors that has helped him survive for so long, and that sets him apart from most other breeds.

Ron Mifratz Haifa (Ron of Haifa Port), one of Prof. Menzel's most influential studs, a consistant producer of good type. This dog was rescued by Prof. Menzel from the SPCA shelter.

One of the most lasting impressions the Canaan gives is of his effortless, ground-eating trot and his strength and agility. This is especially impressive when one considers that so many breeds today are noted for their poor movement.

The short, quick and agile trot of the Canaan, moving towards a single track as he increases his speed, is dependent on the correct structure and shape of body. Faulty construction will inevitably result in incorrect movement. The Canaan should never move in a long lope; he should always look as if he could change direction instantly, leap effortlessly over or onto anything in his path, and keep on going for hours without tiring. From our experience, this is definitely true—Canaans easily run most other breeds into the ground as far as stamina goes.

> **Character:** *Alert, quick to react, distrustful of strangers, strongly defensive but not naturally aggressive. Vigilant not only against man but other animals as well. Extraordinarily devoted and amenable to training.*

Character will be discussed in full in the next chapter—such an important subject deserves a chapter all to itself.

> **Faults:** *All deviations from the standard of the breed. All faults in body structure which constitute a deviation from the norm of a well built dog; anything that would detract from his potential for survival as a desert animal.*
> *N.B.: Male animals should have two apparently normal testicles fully descended into the scrotum.*

C.C.A. Ch. Ariel Shin Ha'aretz of Briel. Bred by Bryna Comsky and Ann Rautenstrauch. Owned by Ellen and Harold Klein, Briel Kennels.

Other Breed Standards

Several countries have written their own breed standards for the Canaan, and we are including them here. However, we feel that the FCI standard, prepared in Israel, the breed's country of origin, by people with many years of experience with the breed, should be the final authority on breed type. We do not feel that clubs in other countries have the right to change the standard to suit the dogs, correct or not, that they have in their area. Rather, they should be trying to breed dogs to suit the standard. For the preservation of the breed, it is important that there be a unified type all over the world, and only the country of origin has the right to set the correct type.

CANAAN CLUB OF AMERICA BREED STANDARD
Adopted: 10 August, 1988

GENERAL APPEARANCE: The Canaan Dog is a herding and flock guardian dog, native to the Middle East. He is aloof with strangers, inquisitive, loyal, and loving with his family. His medium sized, square body is without extremes, showing a clear, sharp outline. The Canaan Dog moves in a quick, brisk, ground covering trot. He has a wedge shaped head with low set prick ears, a bushy tail that curls over the back when excited, and a straight, harsh, close-lying, double coat.

SIZE, PROPORTION AND SUBSTANCE: Dogs 20" to 24", and bitches 19" to 23". Ideal Canaan Dog lies in the middle of the stated ranges. **Disqualification:** Dogs more than 25" or bitches less than 18". **Proportion:** Square. **Substance:** Moderate. Dogs generally weigh 45 to 55 lbs. and bitches approximately 35 to 45 lbs. Dogs distinctly masculine without coarseness and bitches feminine without overrefinement.

HEAD: Elongated, the length exceeding the breadth and depth considerably. Wedge shaped, when viewed from above, blunt, of medium width in the region of the forehead but appearing broader through ears set low to complete an alert expression.

EXPRESSION: Alert, watchful, and inquisitive. Dignified. **Eyes:** Dark, almond shaped, slightly slanted. Varying shades of hazel with liver pointed dogs. Eye rims darkly pigmented or of varying shades of liver, harmonizing to coat color. **Fault:** Unpigmented eye rims. **Ears:** Prick ears. Relatively broad, slightly rounded at the tip. Ears angled very slightly forward when excited. A straight line from the inner corner of the ear to the tip of the nose should just touch the inner corner of the eye and a line drawn from the tip of the ear to the tip of the nose should just touch the outer corner of the eye. Ear motion contibutes to expression and clearly defines the mood of the dog. **Major Fault:** In the adult dog, anything other than prick ears. **Skull:** Slightly arched when viewed from the side, tapering to stop. Slight furrow between the eyes. **Stop:** Slightly accentuated. **Muzzle:** Tapering to complete the wedge shape of the head. Length equal to or slightly longer than the length of the skull from the occiput to stop. Whisker trimming optional. **Nose:** Darkly pigmented or varying shades of liver, harmonizing to coat color. **Lips:** Tight with good pigmentation. **Bite:** Scissors.

NECK, TOPLINE AND BODY: Neck: Well arched. Balanced to body and head and free from throatiness. **Topline:** Straight, slightly sloping from withers to croup. **Body:** Strong, displaying athletic agility and trimness. **Chest:** Moderately broad and deep, extending to the elbows, with well sprung ribs. **Loin:** Well tucked up. Short, muscled flanks. **Tail:** Set on high. Carried curled over the back when excited. Curl ranges from just arched over back to one-and-a-half curl.

FOREQUARTERS: Shoulders: Moderately angulated, angled in to the extent that shoulder blades come within two or three finger widths of each other. **Legs:** Straight. **Pasterns:** Well up. Straight when viewed from the front, flexible with very slight slope when viewed from the side. **Dewclaws:** May be removed. **Feet:** Catlike, pads hard, pigmentation harmonizing with nose and eye rims. **Nails:** Strong, hard, pigmentation harmonizing with either nose and eye rims or coat.

HINDQUARTERS: In balance with forequarters. When viewed from the rear, must be straight. **Thighs:** Musculature well developed, moderately broad. **Hocks:** Well let down. **Dewclaws:** Must be removed. **Feet and Nails:** As in forequarters.

COAT: Straight, close lying, harsh, with slight ruff. Ruff more pronounced on males. **Guard Coat:** ½ to 1½ inches in length; longer on ruff and back of thighs, shorter on body, legs and head. **Undercoat:** Short, density varying with climate. **Tail:** Bushy, increasing in plumage from set to end of bones, then tapering to pointed tip. **Fault:** Excessively long guard coat that masks the clean outline of the dog. Any trimming that alters the natural appearance of the dog.

COLOR: Predominately white with marking(s) of color, or solid colored with or without white trim. Trim may include chest, undercarriage, feet, feet and lower part of leg, and tip of tail. Black, all shades of brown, sandy to reddish, or liver are allowed. Shadings of brown, tan or rust, on a black dog, or black on a brown or tan dog are frequently seen. The solid colored white dog, without a mask as described below, is not allowed. In all color patterns, self colored ticking may be present. **Disqualifications:** Gray and/or brindle as tiger striped. **Mask:** The mask is a desired and distinguishing feature of the predominately white Canaan Dog. The mask is the same color as the body markings on the dog and may contain some black on an otherwise brown dog, or brown on a black dog. The basically symmetrical mask must cover from the rear base of the ears to at least the start of the muzzle and extend down at least onto the cheeks so that the eyes and ears are completely covered. The only allowed white in the mask is a white blaze and/or white on the muzzle below the mask. The blaze may terminate, or vary in width, anywhere along the muzzle or skull, but may not extend over the eye corners. The hooded dog without a blaze is as correct as the dog whose mask and blaze just meet the minimum requirements. A solid colored dog does not have a mask per se, but may have black hairs on the face or white as described above. **Major Fault:** Absence of mask, half mask, or grossly asymmetrical mask on predominantly white dogs.

TEMPERAMENT: Alert, vigilant, devoted and docile with his family. Reserved and aloof with strangers. Highly territorial, serving as a responsive companion and natural guardian. Very vocal, persistent. Easily trained. **Faults:** Shyness or dominance towards people.

KENNEL CLUB OF ENGLAND CANAAN DOG STANDARD
(Interim Standard, Utility Group)

General Appearance: Medium size, well proportioned, of Spitz type.
Characteristics: Versatile and adaptable.
Temperament: Alert, sharp and distrustful of strangers.
Head and Skull: Blunt and wedge shaped. Skull slightly rounded, approximately equal to length of muzzle. Slight stop. Nose preferably dark. Lips clean, tight and well pigmented.
Ears: Set low, prick with broad base and rounded tip.
Eyes: Dark and slightly slanting.
Mouth: Jaws strong with a perfect, regular and complete scissors bite; i.e., upper teeth closely overlapping lower teeth and set square to the jaws.
Neck: Clean, well arched, of medium length.
Forequarters: Forelegs straight, medium boned, shoulders well laid. Pasterns straight and not too short.
Size: Height: 51–61 cms. (20–24 ins.) Weight: 18–25 kgs. (40–45 lbs.) Dogs larger than bitches.
Body: Strong, straight topline with slight slope from withers to croup. Deep brisket, medium breadth of chest, belly well tucked up; loins short and well muscled.

Feet: Round, cat-like with hard pads.

Gait/Movement: Short, fast trot.

Coat: Straight, harsh, medium length; undercoat varying with the season. Legs well feathered, mane desirable in males. Skin of medium thickness and tight to body.

Colour: Sandy to red brown, white or black. Dark and white masks acceptable. Also white markings on body and legs. Grey and black/tan highly undesirable.

Tail: Set high, bushy and carried curled over back.

Hindquarters: Broad, well muscled thighs. Legs straight when viewed from behind with no tendency to cowhocks or bowed hocks. Hocks moderately wide apart and perpendicular to the ground.

Faults: Any departure from the foregoing points should be considered a fault and the seriousness with which the fault should be regarded should be in exact proportion to its degree.

Note: Male animals should have two apparently normal testicles fully descended into the scrotum.

Queen of the Orchid at Morna Vega ("Golda") has won many championships. Isr. Ch. Anan me Shaar Hagai ex Kensix Shenee. Owned by Gina Pointing (England).

Kensix Sheshee, England.

character of
the canaan 4

What most differentiates the Canaan from other breeds is his very typical and quite unique behavior. We have found the same behavior characteristic of the Canaan whether he was born in the wild, or the product of generations of planned breeding; whether raised in the kennel or in the house. Unfortunately, we have noticed a tendency, especially among breeders abroad, to try and change or ignore some of the basic behavior patterns and temperament characteristics of the breed. The Canaan is not an easy breed, nor is he a dog that is suited to everyone. It is important to be very selective in choosing potential puppy owners; people who are not suitable to be Canaan people should be directed to a breed that is more suitable for them. Selectively breeding for a different temperament to give the breed more popular appeal would mean changing some of the most unique and typical characteristics of the breed, characteristics that have ensured the breed's survival and usefulness.

C.C.A. Ch. Ariel Shin Ha'aretz of Briel. Owned by Ellen and Harold Klein, Briel Kennels.

Territoriality

One may consider an extremely developed sense of territoriality as the foundation of the Canaan's character. All dogs, of course, show territoriality (possessiveness toward their "home ground") to a varying degree. In many other breeds, however, this possessiveness is more a function of protecting his *master's* possessions and property. The dog considers the territory an extension of his master and of his responsibility to his master. The Canaan, however, seems to have a different view. He considers the area in which he lives as belonging to *him*, along with all its contents including his "owner." He very quickly learns the boundaries of his property, and although his master may authorize someone to enter or leave or even to bring in or remove something from the property, the Canaan guards it because it is *his*. For this reason, the Canaan is perhaps the best guard in existence for protecting a defined area. He does not need human presence, for once he understands that the area is *his*, he will guard it, whether or not anyone is present.

What makes the Canaan particularly useful as a home guard dog is the way in which he works. The purpose of a watch dog is to be alert, to note anything out of the ordinary, and then to give warning to his master of the presence of something or someone strange, and to give notice of his own presence to any intruders. In most cases, it is not desirable for a home guard dog to be too quick to attack, as many cases that to him look suspicious are only "false alarms." On the other hand, it is a great deterrent to any intruder if a dog begins to cause a great commotion. Any intruder, and particularly a professional criminal, is likely to think twice about facing a dog that is constantly barking and circling out of reach, whereas one of the "attack" breeds, who with a minimum of barking will rush in to bite, is much easier to neutralize, and will attract much less attention. This is the way a Canaan works — he gives very vocal warning of his presence and that he is aware of the intruder, that there is something wrong in his territory and he is notifying all and sundry of the fact, and he circles continuously out of reach, ready to bite only if his warnings are ignored.

In Israel, the Canaan is greatly in demand as a perimeter guard dog for the various security forces. Tests on large numbers of working Canaans and other breeds of working guard dogs have revealed some very interesting facts. The Canaan has been proven to identify a stranger approaching his territory at distances up to five times as great as those at which other breeds identify an approaching person. They have been known to alert at distances as great as one to two kilometers from the approaching intruder in very difficult terrain and under difficult climatic conditions. Other tests have shown that, whereas other breeds will quickly stop barking if the intruder stands still, the Canaans will continue barking as long as the intruder remains in their territory. In addition, if the intruder leaves an object in the territory and retreats, the other dogs will stop barking; the Canaan, however, will continue barking as long as there is anything strange in his territory.

The Canaan will extend his territory if possible. For instance, one of our bitches, brought up as a house dog, began with our yard as her territory, and gradually, as she found no challengers, extended it to the stairs, to the kennel road, and finally to the entire kennel property exclusive only of the yards of neighbors who had dogs of their own. The Canaan immediately recognizes and respects the claim of another dog. A Canaan may feel very insecure when taken out of his own territory. His behavior may be much more passive and less aggressive than it is when he is at home. Some friends of ours who owned a very aggressive Canaan, an outstanding guard dog, were always afraid to take the dog to any of the local dog shows. They were sure that, due to his extreme aggressiveness to other dogs, he would be uncontrollable. They were finally persuaded to try and were amazed at how placid and well behaved the dog was. But of course, for him there was no reason to be aggressive — he was outside of his own territory.

Dogs mark their territory, urinating at selected spots along the perimeter to leave "scent posts" for other dogs, defining their property. This is common among males of all breeds. However, in Canaans, the bitches are just as territorial as the males and they will also scent mark their territory, actually lifting their legs and urinating in numerous spots along the perimeter — quite a unique behavior pattern among domestic breeds.

Alertness

The Canaan is notable for his extreme alertness. All of his senses are unusually well developed. Even his eyesight is particularly keen, perhaps nearly as keen as the eyesight of the sighthounds. The Canaan

Briels' Geva Shoshanna Shirah. Owned by William and Lorraine Stephens.

will alert to someone approaching and give warning long before other dogs seem to be aware of the possible intrusion. His sense of smell is also very sharp. Canaans have been successfully trained for varied tracking tasks, and seem to be able to continue on a track in hot and dry weather conditions that interfere with the effective work of dogs of other breeds.

As Canaans do feel the need to protect their territory from the intrusion of other animals as well as of humans, the Canaan is also very likely to alert and start to bark at the presence of other dogs, cats, or other animals. It is important to educate the Canaan from a young age to what you want him to alert to, and to discourage him from unnecessary barking to prevent his becoming a nuisance.

Suspicion

Except for the few people that he knows, loves and respects, the Canaan Dog regards the rest of the world with great suspicion. Any new acquaintances must prove themselves worthy of his attention. He does not like to be touched by strangers, and will inspect anyone new while staying just out of reach. He is also suspicious of any changes in his surroundings, his daily routine, and so on. He is suspicious of strange food; there has been little success in attempts by the veterinary services in their rabies control program to destroy wild packs of Canaans through use of poisoned bait—the animals will not pick it up. Attempts to neutralize guard dogs with poisoned tidbits have also failed—the dogs have been found alert at their posts with the poisoned bait untouched.

As an example of this suspiciousness, a kennel-raised bitch was loaned to Tel Aviv University for measurements of water requirements. There she was kenneled in facilities very similar to her home. After several days, we were notified that she wouldn't eat. They had been trying to feed her fresh meat when she had been accustomed to eating dry, concentrated dog food. Since the meat was strange to her, she wouldn't touch it. It was necessary for me to go to the kennel and offer her the meat by hand, showing her that it was all right. She then ate it with pleasure.

Canaans that grow up and live in isolated surroundings may be extremely suspicious to the point of being totally unwilling to approach anyone other than their master, while dogs brought up in town, with a great deal of exposure to a variety of people, places, and experiences will be much more willing to accept and make friends with strangers. Some of our dogs that have a great deal of experience travelling and appearing at dog shows are very friendly to people that approach them when they are with us. When they are in their own territory and approached by strangers, without being "introduced," they are as effective as watch dogs and as suspicious as any dog with less experience.

It is however, very important for puppies and young dogs to get as much socialization as possible to develop their self-confidence and their ability to cope effectively with strange people and surroundings. Many puppies go through a period of "hyper-suspiciousness" at some time between five months to one and a half years of age. As they mature and gain more self confidence, this over-suspiciousness tends to disappear. Obedience training during this period helps to give them more confidence and a better framework for handling this suspiciousness.

The Canaan should not be punished for being suspicious or standoffish — this can be traumatic for him and make the situation worse. He should be treated in a way that shows him that he can trust and depend on you, and should be encouraged in behavior that shows a developing self-confidence.

Aggressiveness

The Canaan is by nature aggressive to other dogs. He will without hesitation attack any strange dog invading his territory. Males will take on other males and bitches other bitches. It is important to note that bitches are not any less territorial and aggressive to other dogs than males. Fights over territory, food, and even dominance between a dog and a bitch are not uncommon. Whereas in most breeds dog fights end when one of the combatants acknowledges his subordinance, with Canaans a fight may continue to the death of one participant. Fights between bitches may be particularly bitter. Canaans can live together in groups only when they have worked out a very precise "pecking order" among themselves.

However, the Canaan will rarely show aggression to defenseless animals, unless they are hunting them for food. The Canaans are widely kept by Bedouin, by Arab villagers, and by farmers, and protect the livestock effectively without attempting to harass it; this includes sheep

Ch. Laish me Bnei HaBitachon at work.

with their newborn lambs, cattle, and various barnyard fowl. We have, however, observed aggression to animals that they consider dangerous, including lizards and poisonous snakes. One bitch succeeded in killing large vipers on three occasions. Her speed was phenomenal. She grabbed the snake before it could strike, flipped it into the air, and in the same motion jumped out of reach. She kept returning, always approaching from behind, trying for a hold behind the head. As the snake weakened, she did get a hold behind the head, shook it until it was dead, and then buried it.

The Canaan will be aggressive to humans only if he feels he has reason, and for him the reason may be ignoring his warnings. He will bite to protect his territory if his warning barking is not heeded and if the intruder appears threatening. He may bite to defend his own rights or his position in the "pack." We have had a Canaan male show aggressive tendencies when a bitch that had been living together with him in one kennel, or that had been put in with him for breeding, was taken out. Canaan bitches may be quite aggressive in defense of their puppies. When the dog has been allowed, over an extended period of time, to develop the feeling that he is the "pack leader" in the household, he may bite to defend his food or when he objects to being made to do something. For the most part, aggressiveness in the domestic Canaan is controlled by his respect for people in general and "his" people in particular.

The Canaan is never aggressive without reason; however, what he considers a good reason is not necessarily what you would consider as such. Basic obedience training is highly recommended to provide a control framework that the dog will understand.

Loyalty and Devotion

The Canaan is extremely loyal and devoted to those he loves. However, his relationship with his master differs from that of most other breeds of dog. For him, it is a partnership, with both sides giving affection and devotion, but with both sides also having their "own life." The Canaan does not feel it necessary to spend all his time following his master around. He may come into the house for a few hours, show great affection, seek attention and petting, and then ask to be let out so that he can "go about his own affairs." He rarely follows his master from room to room; however, although he may not feel the necessity to follow him, he is always aware of exactly where his master is and what he is doing. The Canaan requires affection and care from his master and in exchange returns devotion and the desire to guard and protect him, but he always retains his basic independence. He belongs to no one but himself.

He is not a "one man dog," but is devoted to the entire family. If raised with children, he is very gentle and considerate of them, and develops a great attachment and affection for them. He also tends to be extremely protective of the children of the family.

Katzefet sings.

A typical Canaan pose.

Eleven-week-old puppy.

43

Although the Canaan is independent, he is not a wanderer. His desire for personal independence does not result in his leaving his property, in contrast to many breeds noted for their wanderlust or their tendency to follow their noses and forget where they are going. The Canaan simply prefers to decide for himself when he feels he would like attention or companionship, and not be forced into anything. He likes to make his own decisions.

Adaptability

In our experience with the Canaan, we have frequently been amazed by his great adaptability to all kinds of conditions and changes. We have seen Canaans living well and happily as kennel dogs, as farm dogs with unlimited space in which to run, as apartment dogs whose only activity was a short walk twice a day, and under many other conditions. We have had wild Canaans, captured as adults, adjust unbelievably quickly to being domesticated pets. We have seen house dogs adjust with no problem to living in the kennels. Great variations in diet and care don't phase them; their extremely efficient metabolism makes effective use of whatever they are provided with. Canaans have also been proven to adapt to wide extremes of climate with no problems, exemplified by dogs that have been sent to places such as Canada or Finland. None of the other domestic breeds with which we have had experience could adapt as well to such a great variety of conditions as the Canaan.

Intelligence

The Canaan is highly intelligent. His intelligence is that of an animal who has been required to depend on it to survive. He can be easily trained to most tasks, and is a good worker on lead, but due to his native independence and tendency to think for himself, he can be unreliable when off lead. As with most intelligent breeds, he tends to be bored by routine obedience work, although if he is working at a task that he enjoys or that presents a challenge, he will work very well. Canaans learn very quickly, and I have seen them learn from observation as well.

The Canaan is also very good at demonstrating just how adept he is at problem solving by figuring out how to escape from pens, through fences and so on, or by showing up his master in other ways.

Other Characteristic Behavior

No description of the Canaan is complete without a mention of his passion for digging holes. The Canaan is not a destructive puppy, rarely chews up things around the house, and doesn't have difficulty in learning to be house clean. But no matter under what conditions he lives, if a Canaan has a chance, he will dig. No self-respecting Canaan will use a dog house if he can dig a hole under it. No home belonging to a Canaan can be found without a few "Canaani holes" in the garden. We have often taken Canaans to dog shows, left them tied under a tree until time for judging, and found that after a short time they have dug themselves a very comfortable hole. These holes can be quite elaborate — quite big enough for the dog himself, and sometimes real caves. (In one case, a puppy bitch dug a hole under the leg of the hot water heater which resulted in the whole thing collapsing.) There are few breeds that take such pleasure in digging, or that really put their digging to use as does the Canaan.

In addition to digging holes, the Canaan also likes to bury things. If he is not hungry and has a chance, he will bury his extra food. We have also had dogs that buried not only the extra food, but the food dish as well. One never knows when hard times might come.

Most breeds when at rest like to lie flat on their sides, and many dogs even roll over and lie on their backs with their feet in the air. Not the Canaan. He doesn't sleep in such exposed positions. He curls himself into a tight ball, usually with his forepaws between his hind legs and his tail curled over his nose. Puppies like to lie inside things; it is common to find them curled up inside their food dishes.

The Canaan is an extremely clean animal by nature. He always tries to keep his surroundings clean, and is thus very easy to housetrain. He is also very good at keeping himself free of parasites, and rarely has fleas or ticks, except perhaps in the ears or on the neck where he cannot reach them to remove them.

Lifespan

The average lifespan of the Canaan is still something we are not sure of — they seem to be very long lived dogs. We know that many Canaans at the age of ten, twelve, or older are still fully alert, in excellent physical condition, and still happily filling their guard dog duties. We have seen dogs in Bedouin camps, where life is difficult to say the least, that, according to the Bedouin, were fifteen or more. The Bedouin kept track of the age by relating it to the age of a child born to them at the time the puppy was born or obtained. We have had dogs reach seventeen and eighteen years, and have seen one over twenty years of age that was in excellent condition, alert and still able to guard.

Int. It. Ch. W.W. 1991 Edom Beit Kuti (left) and Int. It. Ch. W.W. 1992 Lilith me Shaar Hagai (right).

caring for
your dog   5

Food and Water Requirements

The Canaan Dog in the natural state subsisted very well on very little. Unlike most of our pampered modern breeds who seem to require all kinds of special care as far as diet and supplements go, the Canaan got along on what he could catch through his own hunting, and what he could scavenge in the rubbish heaps, fringes of settlements, and Bedouin camps. Despite the chancy diet, most Canaans seen in the wild or around Bedouin camps were well developed and in overall good condition.

We have, over the years, found definite indications that the Canaan requires comparatively less food for his size and is much more adaptable to changes in diet than other breeds. The Canaans have done very well over the years on a wide variety of diets dictated by local conditions, commercial complete feeds, and homemade diets.

During the Yom Kippur War of 1973, we involuntarily did "research" on the food requirements and food adaptability of the Canaan as compared to other breeds. Ordinary commercial dog food was not available and we were forced to improvise, making use of materials at hand, such as soya meal, bone meal, bread, milk powder and so on. We had a large number of other dogs of various breeds in boarding at the time and almost all lost some weight and condition, some even a good deal, on the improvised diet. Only the Canaans remained in peak condition, at their proper weight, with healthy glossy coats, and gave all indications of sufficient nutrition.

We have found that the Canaan does very well on a good quality commercial complete diet, requiring 200 to 300 grams per day only to remain in fine condition. However, a Canaan can get along on many other diets just as well, as long as the diet is balanced to provide his basic nutritional requirements.

The Canaan also requires less water than other breeds. This is doubtless a result of their adaptation and development in a semi-desert to desert environment. This, of course, was to be expected. But as we began to suspect very real differences in water requirements, we began to watch for specific instances. Various observations by ourselves and also by several university research teams proved that the Canaan drinks less and makes more efficient use of water than other breeds.

The Bedouin, of course, recognized this fact long ago. The Canaan went out with the goats and sheep, who were grazed far from water all day and brought back only in the evening to drink; sometimes they had access to water only once in two days. The Canaan drank when the flock drank. The Salukis were left in the home tents as they had difficulty going for so long without water.

We are not, of course, advising you to leave your Canaan without water. Like any other dog, he should always have a dish of water available. However, his minimal water requirement is one of the things that sets him apart from other breeds.

Three and a half month puppies of lovely type. Left, Hamah me Shaar Hagai. Right, Sirpad me Shaar Hagai.

Alisa me Ofra at 16 years of age, still shows alert, correct expression.

Grooming

The Canaan is a very clean dog by nature and requires very little extra care. His short harsh coat is easy to care for and requires little grooming. Most of the year, a brisk brushing once or twice a week will keep him in good condition. During shedding season, he sheds out his thick woolly undercoat in great clumps; he should then be brushed every day or even twice a day to remove all this dead hair. This will keep him from getting itchy and uncomfortable, will encourage the new coat to come in faster, and will more quickly end the inconvenience of shedding around the house. He rarely needs to be bathed, unless he has been rolling in something particularly smelly. A completely natural dog, he needs no trimming or plucking.

The Canaan has very strong nails that grow rapidly. When the dog does not have enough activity to wear them down, they must be cut fairly frequently. (In the wild, the Canaans need strong long nails for digging their dens, and for digging after small prey). Canaans often object strongly to the idea of having their nails cut, at times very vocally, but can be trained to patiently endure this necessary procedure.

The Canaan usually keeps himself fairly free of external parasites. However, if your area is infested with ticks or fleas, it is advisable to powder him regularly with a good commercial product during the parasite season. Most Canaans are not particularly sensitive or prone to skin irritations or eczemas, although we have known of a few who developed an allergic eczema to flea bites.

Training

The Canaan is a highly intelligent dog and quickly learns what is expected of him, including the behavior required if he is to be a comfortable companion. Clean by nature, he has no difficulty in acquiring the principles of being clean in the house — his basic instincts lead him to seek a place to "do his business" as far as possible from his living quarters.

He is amenable to obedience training and picks up the basic exercises with ease. However, one thing to keep in mind when training the Canaan is to vary the routine and the exercises he is working on. Being an extremely intelligent and independent animal, he will quickly get bored with having to repeat the same exercises over and over, especially since he will probably have grasped the principle involved after the first few tries. If the exercises are varied and he is often presented with new and challenging tasks, he will keep up his interest and work better and more willingly.

With the Canaan, it is always worthwhile to keep in mind that he is not your servant, but your partner in work. For this reason, although he may quickly reach a stage where he is very reliable working on lead, there are times when he may not be reliable off lead, for instance if he feels that other things are more demanding of his attention. By building a good working partnership with your dog and keeping him interested in his work, this problem can, for the most part, be overcome.

Some Canaans are quite dominant and during the training period may challenge the trainer's authority by disobeying deliberately, or even growling at corrections. It is very important in these instances for the trainer to display his dominance over the dog by making the dog obey the command and submit to the trainer's authority. However, discipline should never be cruel or overly aggressive — with the Canaan, this kind of behavior tends to arouse his instincts of self-defense. Canaans respond best to being corrected in "dog language," such as being grabbed by the scruff of the neck and shaken, or being flattened to the ground in submissive posture. This demonstrates very well who is the pack leader.

A great deal of satisfaction can be derived from working together with your dog. Canaans have been successfully trained to a wide variety of activities, including all levels of obedience work (in which they have competed successfully in all-breed competition), tracking, patrol work, herding, hunting, and several have been trained as guide dogs for the blind. Training and working with your Canaan will develop the relationship between you and your dog, and bring both of you to a more rewarding partnership and mutual understanding.

It is best to start training basic commands in a gentle way from the day the new puppy arrives home, so that he will grow up with the idea of obedience and acceptance of your authority. We recommend joining organized obedience classes when the puppy is five to six months old.

Terramara's Achad, owned and bred by Terry Bagley. Sire: Padre's Shekvar von Karstadt. Dam: Southalta's Beriah.

We will not go into specific training methods here as there are many excellent books available that explain dog training step by step, as well as the group training courses available in most areas.

Health

The Canaan is, by nature, a very healthy and hardy dog. Being still very close to his wild ancestors, where the rule was survival of the fittest, he is a very fit breed that requires no special care and is not prone to diseases or weaknesses. A Canaan, properly cared for, is likely to go through life never requiring the services of a veterinarian other than for routine vaccinations.

There is one exception, however, and that is parvovirus. Parvovirus appeared in dogs only a decade or so ago. It is a virulent gastrointestinal virus that most frequently attacks puppies, is extremely debilitating, and in a significant number of instances results in death. We have found the Canaan puppy to be particularly susceptible to this disease, likely to become infected if exposed, and with a high percentage of puppies not surviving once they have contracted the disease. On the other hand, we know of almost no cases of a Canaan over five or six months of age contracting parvovirus. There is a vaccination available for parvovirus and we strongly advise vaccinating puppies at a young age and then periodically until they reach six or eight months of age. Subsequently, a booster should be given once a year. Young puppies should also be kept at home, and not exposed to strange dogs or places where strange dogs have passed, where there may be a danger of infection.

Canaan puppies, and all breeds, should be vaccinated with the DHL vaccine (Distemper, Hepatitis, and Leptospirosis). This is done between two and three months of age, with one or two boosters a month apart, and then annually. At the age of four months your Canaan puppy should be vaccinated against rabies; this is also repeated once a year.

We also find it advisable to routinely worm the dogs once or twice a year. Your vet can advise you as to worming and what to use; he can also test the dog's stools to see if worming is necessary.

Other than taking proper care of your dog, it is advisable to find a reliable veterinarian and to follow his instructions as to general health and treatment in case of specific health problems. Do not hesitate to call on your vet for advice if for any reason you feel that your dog is ill. Symptoms to watch for are lethargy, loss of appetite, runny eyes and nose, rise in temperature (the dog's normal temperature is 38 C or 101.5 F), vomiting or abnormal stools, or other abnormal behavior. Should these symptoms occur, consult an expert immediately.

Canaans are not prone to hereditary diseases and defects such as hip dysplasia, epilepsy, eye and ear defects. For years we have done hip X-rays of breeding stock up to the age of twelve or thirteen years of age in order to verify our belief that this problem is not prevalent in the Ca-

CCA Ch. Lahatut me Shaar Hagai Ud.

naan. In our years of X-raying, we have had no Canaans with signs of hip-dysplasia or deterioration of the hip joint, even at a very advanced age.

There have been some problems with patella luxation. However, once the problem appeared, an effort was made to remove related animals from the breeding program, and over the last years there have been no signs of a recurrence of the problem.

Showing

Dog shows can be a lot of fun for both you and your dog, but your dog must be in peak condition and trained to behave properly in the ring and on the show grounds so that all can enjoy the experience.

As the Canaan is a natural dog, no special preparations are involved in taking him to a dog show. He does not need trimming, plucking or special grooming. To be in show condition, your dog must be healthy and fit, not too thin or too fat, muscular, with a clean shiny coat. His nails should be trimmed short enough so that they don't touch the ground when he walks. His ears and teeth should be clean.

Your dog should be trained to walk properly on a loose lead at your left side, with his head level with your knee, without pulling forward or dragging behind. It is important that the dog gait smoothly so that the judge can evaluate his movement. He must stand naturally and squarely when you stop, and should be prepared to stand at the alert, with ears and tail up, at a signal from you. In most countries you are allowed to "bait" your dog in the show ring (bring him to the alert by teasing him with a tasty tidbit). However, he should not start leaping around trying to grab the bait.

Your dog must be prepared to allow the judge examine him, and must allow you to lift his lips so that the judge can check his teeth and bite. If he is a male, the judge will also check his testicles. Many Canaans are not happy about having a stranger approach and handle them, especially when it is also in a strange place and with many other dogs and people around, so practice with your dog in advance, preferably with the help of friends to do the examining, so that he will know what to expect. In many areas, ring training classes are held by breed or local canine societies. It is a very good idea to join such a class and give your dog (and yourself!) experience and training before attending an actual show. Many Canaans very much enjoy showing themselves off and receiving attention once they have been trained. A dog show can be a rewarding experience for you and your dog.

There are several different systems of showing. In the U.S. and Canada, dogs can be entered in one or more of a number of classes offered, which include Puppy (6-9 months), Puppy (9-12 months), Novice,

Isr. Ch. W.W. 1985 Ra'anana me Shaar Hagai, winning group 1, Tel Aviv Int. Show 1989.

American Bred, Bred by Exhibitor, and Open. In each class (which are divided by sex — bitches are judged only with bitches and dogs with dogs), the judge chooses a first, second, third, and fourth place. The first place winner from each class then enters Winner's Class, where the judge chooses Winners Dog and Winners Bitch, and a Reserve Winners Dog and Reserve Winners Bitch. If this is an official point show, Winners Dog and Winners Bitch are the recipients of the points towards championship. In the United States a dog must earn 15 points to become a champion; part of these points must be at major shows where at least three points are awarded. (The points awarded are according to the number of dogs that compete.) The winners then compete with the Specials (Champions), if there are any in competition, for the title of Best of Breed and Best of Opposite Sex. In the U.S. and Canada, the judge "places" the dogs with no written or oral comments on them. The Canaan is now recognized by the kennel clubs of both countries and can be shown in official point shows.

In the FCI member countries, including Israel, there are only three official classes for dogs and for bitches — Youth Class, 9-15 months; Open Class, over 15 months; and Champion Class, for a dog with a national or international championship title. Each dog is judged individually by the judge and is rated on a scale from "Excellent" to "Insufficient." The judge must provide a written report on each dog he judges. All "Excellent" dogs in each class then compete for first, second and third place. In the Youth Class, the judge may award the title Youth Winner; in Open Class, if it is a Championship show, the judge may award the CAC (candidacy for national championship) if he feels the first place dog is worthy of it; otherwise he may withhold the title. At an International show, he may award the CACIB (candidacy for International Champion) to the dog he feels is best out of the Open and Champion classes. If he feels no dog is of sufficient quality, the award may be withheld. If in any class the judge is not satisfied with the quality of the dogs, he may withhold all placements — this is not uncommon in the FCI system. The winners of all classes compete for Best of Breed and Best of Opposite Sex.

Every country of the FCI has its own requirements for awarding the national Championship title. In Israel, to become a Champion, the dog must win three CACs at three different shows under at least two different judges. To become an FCI International Champion, the dog must win four CACIBs in at least three countries from at least three different judges in a period of at least a year and a day.

In England and South Africa, there are also several classes that can be entered, and in each class there are four places. At a championship show, the winners of the CC (Challenge Certificates–Candidacy for Championship) are chosen from the winners of the classes (one from each sex). Additional honors that are awarded are Best of Breed and Best of Opposite Sex. In England and South Africa, a finished Champion may

be awarded additional CCs. The judges are not required to make written or oral reports on the dogs they judge. They are also entitled to
withhold CCs.

**Briel's Dinah Bat Gvir was bred by Ellen Minto. She won first place in a Junior
Showmanship class with Brooke Leyen in Fremont, Nebraska, June 3, 1995.**

Arad me Shaar Hagai, CCA Ch. with two daughters: Terramara's Behak, CCA Ch., CCA CD; and Terramara's Caleh, CCA Ch; and one son, Terramara's Ezrada, CCA Ch. (Canada) (left to right).

Hila me Shaar Hagai won best of breed and a group 1 at Friends of Waterloo Kennel Club Rare Breed Show on August 7, 1994.

breeding   6

Most unique about the Canaan are the behavior patterns of breeding, whelping and the raising of puppies. Their behavior during these periods is a clear expression of their closeness to nature and the dictates of its laws.

Trapper ex Hila puppies at 4 weeks of age, whelped October 10, 1994.

Managing the stud dog

Whereas males in many breeds will show great interest in bitches and successfully breed even at nine or ten months of age, we have found that it is very common in the Canaan male that he shows no great interest or drive to breed before he is 1½ to 2 years old, and sometimes not until considerably later. We consider this an indication of their closeness to the behavior common in wild packs of canines. In the pack, only a fully mature male, at the height of his physical development and capable of holding his own against the other males in the pack, will feel secure enough to attempt to gain himself bitches and to breed. The younger and less developed males are apparently protected by nature by not developing a powerful sex drive until they are physically capable of challenging the other males in the pack. Shaar Hagai's foundation stud dog, Isr. Ch. Laish me Bnei HaBitachon, sire of many litters, was quite an uninterested and indifferent stud until he was close to four years old.

We have, over the last several years, had some exceptions, where young dogs of about a year of age have been extremely interested and successful in breeding. These were dogs with very dominant personalities; because of their strong temperaments, they were raised in their own kennels, often in the company of a bitch. Apparently, having his "own" property, and his "own" bitch, was enough to convince a young, strong dog that he was mature enough to take on all comers, especially as he was able to "fight" with his neighbors, (through the fence) without risk of injury, or of being "put down" by the other dogs.

Adult Canaan males, especially once they have started to breed, can rarely be kept together with another male; they must have their own territory, and they can become extremely possessive about a bitch they have bred.

A word of advice—not every male must be a stud dog. Contrary to popularly held opinion, not every male must have a chance to breed to be healthy and happy. On the contrary, a male who is not going to be used regularly as a stud, who might be a marvelous pet and companion but isn't of such high quality that he can make an important contribution to the breed through his offspring, is better off never breeding. His sex drive will be less developed if he has no breeding experience, and he will be less likely to try to go off looking for bitches.

In deciding whether or not to breed your male, always take into consideration whether he is of high enough quality so that his puppies will have a good chance of being even better breed examples. Never breed an animal of less than top quality, as this way you are proliferating less desirable qualities in the breed. Instead, enjoy him as a pet and companion.

If your male is of breeding quality, and you find that there are owners of suitable bitches interested in using him, the next step is the mating itself. First of all, don't feel that it is necessary to accept all bitches that are suggested for breeding to your dog. The bitch should be complementary in quality to the qualities of your dog, and the two should never have common faults. Usually, it is a good idea to have an experienced bitch for your dog's first breeding. The two should be allowed to get acquainted—ideally in a closed yard or pen, where they can sniff one another and then run around and play for some time. Canaans do have a play ritual connected with breeding, and without the chance to proceed with this behavior pattern, the breeding may not succeed as either the dog or bitch may refuse to cooperate. Once the dog begins mounting the bitch, and making a serious attempt to penetrate, the bitch's owner should be prepared to hold her, to prevent her from moving away or turning to snap at the dog. An over-aggressive bitch, or a bitch brought on the wrong day of her heat when she is not willing to accept the dog, and when she will likely be aggressive about it, can be a very bad experience for a young inexperienced dog, and may even put him off from trying other breedings in the future.

Once the dog has succeeded in penetrating the bitch, hold him on her back for a moment, and then assist him gently to get down and turn around in the natural position (rump to rump). The dog and bitch are now in what is called a tie; during this whole period, semen is passing from the dog to the bitch. This may last from a few minutes to as much as an hour; average is about 15 to 20 minutes. At the completion, the dog and bitch will separate themselves. (Don't try to "help"!)

It is advisable to repeat a breeding after 48 hours, to be sure of catching the bitch's fertile days.

The dog owner should be sure to make all arrangements in connection with his stud fee in advance of the breeding; it should also be agreed between dog and bitch owners what is to happen in case of an unsuccessful mating—will the stud owner grant a repeat breeding without charge or at a reduced rate or at all? What if there are only one or two puppies in the litter? Stud fees may range from the pick puppy of the litter to a cash fee.

Managing the brood bitch

Most Canaan bitches have their first heat at about 8 to 14 months of age. It is very rare for a Canaan female to have her first heat as early as 6 months—the bitch is usually well developed and mature enough physically by the time of her first heat to adequately deal with the demands of a litter in the wild. Most Canaan bitches come in heat on a cycle of six to eight months between heats, but, (as will be discussed later on), the Canaan's cycle is much more subject to the influences of natural conditions than is the case in other breeds.

Canaan bitches are very clean when in heat, to the point where it is often quite difficult to spot the beginning days, as there are no blood spots around.

Isr. Ch. Zaaka me Shaar Hagai (Ch. Dardar me Shaar Hagai ex Petra Hamuvcheret me Shaar Hagai). A top winning bitch with several group placements, a fine working dog, and an outstanding producer. Several of her offspring are winning abroad.

The heat period averages about 21 days, and the norm is that the bitch is ready to breed on about day 10 to 12 until about day 17. There can be wide individual variations, however—we have had bitches ready to breed in the first few days of the heat, and one bitch bred on day 21. The best indications of when your bitch is ready are: when the vulval discharge changes from blood red to a pale straw color, the vulva becomes very swollen and soft to the touch, and the bitch "flags," that is, moves her tail completely to the side when touched in the vicinity of the vulva.

Canaan bitches will by preference choose Canaan males as their mates. They seem very definitely to be able to differentiate between themselves and other breeds of dog, much more than any other breeds in my experience. We have often seen bitches in a wild or semi-wild state rejecting "suitors" of other breeds and choosing Canaan males. There is the example of one bitch that was sold to a kibbutz member. Although locked up when she came in heat, she escaped, and did not choose to breed to any of the kibbutz dogs. She disappeared and was later found in a Bedouin camp some kilometers away, with a lovely Canaan male that she had chosen as her mate.

Canaan bitches do exhibit preferences as to their mate, and seem to have a tendency, if allowed, to prefer one permanent mate. Pairs can become very devoted to one another, and will suffer if separated. They

60

enjoy playing together, but even when the bitch is in heat, and males and females are being kept in pairs, we rarely observe any mounting behavior until the days when the bitch is actually ready to breed. From the behavior of the pairs, it is rarely possible to tell that a bitch is in heat until she actually is ready to accept the male. Bitches in the wild will usually refuse to accept more than one dog as mate during the heat period; this is testified to by Bedouins we have talked with. Despite the fact that there are numbers of males pursuing a bitch, the Bedouin know which dog is the sire of the litter and state that the bitch refused other dogs.

Another interesting point which we have observed over the years and which is indicative of the Canaan's closeness to nature is the possible connection of fertility in the Canaan bitch with the conditions of climate. We do not have enough actual data on this to make any conclusive statement, but, at this stage, can only present our impression. We have seen a number of Canaan bitches in a normal appearing heat and with no change in their normal cycle, refuse to accept any male; other bitches who did accept males, and even bitches allowed to breed freely during their entire "ready" period, did not conceive. These occurrences were all within a period of several months during the summer and fall of a year following several years of severe drought. The drought subsequently continued through the following winter—thus, in the wild, conditions would have been adverse to raising a litter. (Some of these bitches were wild born, but most were from several generations of "domesticated" stock.) The next summer and fall, most of these bitches were tried again, bred normally, conceived, and whelped normal litters—some of the litters were even unusually large. The drought broke that winter.

We have also seen bitches who normally have a cycle of six to eight months come in heat every three to four months in a good year (that is, a year with plentiful rain), until they are bred.

Whelping and maternal care

The gestation period is 63 days, but may vary from 59 to 65 days. Canaan bitches are particularly easy whelpers. Unlike most other dogs, the Canaan bitch gives little advance warning of when she intends to whelp. Most bitches of other breeds will go through a prolonged period of restlessness, panting, scratching up their "nest" area, refusing to eat, and so on. A Canaan bitch, even when whelping her first litter, may eat a hearty meal and appear perfectly comfortable, and then in an hour or so begin producing puppies.

The whelping itself in most cases proceeds with great ease. With the many litters we have whelped over the last 12 years, it was very rare for a bitch to need assistance of any sort. Bitches whelping for the first time might be a bit nervous, but never to the point of the hysteria not uncommon in some other breeds. The Canaan bitch is always capable of coping with the proper cleaning of the puppies, the nest and herself.

Canaan puppies at 4 weeks of age, with Bertha Sheaffer of Spatterdash Kennels. Sire: Aleph of Star Pine; Dam: Waf of Massada.

We have also never had a Canaan bitch become overly upset or nervou and sit on her own puppies.

Whelping is generally completed in a fairly short period of time Although the average litters is 5 to 8 puppies, we have had bitches deliver as many as ten or twelve puppies in two to three hours.

Canaan puppies at birth are unusually large in relationship to the size of the bitch. In some cases, the total weight of a Canaan litter would be in the vicinity of 20 percent of the dam's normal body weight. This trait may be explained as a desert survival factor—the large size of the pups at birth compensates for the tendency to weight loss from dehydration in the first day or two of life. It is not uncommon for other desert mammal species to be born comparatively larger than non-desert living members of the same family—apparently for this reason. Observation indicates less fluid making up the birth weight than in other breeds. It also appears that a larger percentage of Canaan puppies are born with the birth sac intact, whereupon the mother breaks the sac and immediately licks up the fluid again, while in other breeds the sac is frequently broken, and the fluid not reingested.

Canaan bitches are extremely clean about the whelping. We have never had a Canaan bitch whose nest, self and puppies were not spotless at the conclusion of the whelping. Canaan bitches will go to the extent of attempting to eat stillborn puppies in an effort to clean the nest.

Canaan puppies are usually born without dewclaws, but occasionally we will have puppies born with them; in such cases we remove them

A bitch in a den she has dug for whelping under an old barrel.

on the second or third day. We had one case of a Canaan bitch who herself removed the dewclaws on her newborn puppies by biting them off.

Any Canaan bitch that was kept in an earth floored pen, or was allowed to run free prior to whelping, whether house pet, generations removed from the wild, or wild born, would dig herself a den in which to whelp. Dens like this are very standard in construction—a deep hole large enough for the bitch to turn around in comfortably, usually underneath a rock or tree, reached by a down sloping passage which turns to the left to connect to the den. The down slope is at an angle which is conducive to puppies climbing up at a very young age to eliminate and then being able to roll and slide back down into the den.

The den is extremely secure—because of the bend, it is impossible for predators or anyone else to reach the bitch and pups, and the bitch is able to completely protect her pups by closing off the entrance with her body. We have seen identical dens among wild Canaans and Bedouin dogs. In several cases we made attempts to get the bitch out, and found it impossible.

Canaan bitches are very careful and devoted mothers. Bitches of other breeds may be excellent mothers, but by the time their puppies are five or six weeks old, they generally begin to lose patience and would be glad to be rid of them. They are usually no longer nursing the puppies, or if so, minimally, and prefer to "get away" from them as much as possible. The Canaan bitch, however will go on nursing and caring for her puppies for a long time. Bitches left with their litters will commonly nurse them until two or three months of age. She will continue cleaning the nest as long as necessary; we have had bitches cleaning up after their puppies up to two and a half to three months of age, when the puppies were eating four solid meals a day. Canaan puppies, from a very young age when given the opportunity, will leave the nest to eliminate. Canaan bitches frequently regurgitate for their puppies, even to their own detriment. It is sometimes necessary to separate a Canaan bitch from her puppies, just to keep the bitch from depleting her own reserves from overmuch devotion.

The Canaan bitch seems to have an urge not only to care physically for her offspring, but also to educate them. Bitches allowed to remain with their puppies appear definitely to be teaching them. Unfortunately for us, with the Canaans, some of the primary teaching seems to be climbing fences, digging holes, and escaping from pens! I spent several months in "ambush," observing one bitch allowed to run free, whose puppies (at this point four or five months old) we attempted to keep penned. The bitch would either jump into the pen or circle the perimeter until she found a "weak point," and would then "show" her puppies how to get over, under or through at that point. Every time I repaired one spot, she would show them another. This bitch would also take her puppies out into the surrounding forest, leave them there, come back, and sit watching the forest and waiting for them to return. She was obviously teaching them how to get along. The bitch also teaches her puppies, through her example, how to react to the surrounding world.

Puppy development

Canaan puppies develop very quickly—this extremely rapid development and unusually early agility, coordination and independence is one of the things that most sets them apart from other breeds. Their development to self-sufficiency is more rapid than in any other breed I have observed.

We start offering the puppies solid food, in addition to their dam's milk, at three weeks of age. Usually their introduction to food consists of porridge, white cheese (cream or cottage cheese), sometimes diluted a bit with water, or dog kibble soaked until it is soft. However, Canaan puppies will often begin stealing food from their mother's dish even earlier, and at a very young age cope with dry kibble and other food stuffs that small puppies of other breeds would find very difficult to eat.

Canaan puppies possess very strong instincts of cleanliness—from as early as three weeks of age they will use only one corner of their nest for elimination, and if in a box, den or dog house that they can get out of, they will start crawling out of their living quarters to eliminate. We had a litter of puppies kept with their dam in a pen with wide-gauge fencing. These puppies, from about four weeks of age, could crawl through the fence to eliminate outside of their pen. We have had other bitches and puppies that would squeeze out under the door of their kennel, a height of about 8 centimeters, to eliminate outside of their living area. (Until we actually observed some of this, we couldn't believe that the dogs could possibly have managed to get out of the kennels that way!) It was obvious in such cases that the bitch was teaching her puppies to avoid soiling their living area.

Canaan puppies develop physical control over their bodies and coordination much earlier than other breeds. The Canaan puppy at four to five weeks of age is already a small dog—he is active, coordinated, alert and aware, while pups of other breeds are still stumbling over their own feet. Canaans at this age are frequently already climbing to the roof of their dog house—a height of about one meter. They climb up the fence wire in a corner next to the dog box, with their backs pressed against the box as support, quite a unique system. By about 6 weeks, it becomes very difficult to keep Canaans in an average puppy pen—they climb out, dig under, or find some hole or space to squeeze through.

Aggressiveness and possessiveness also develop in the Canaan pup at a very young age. As early as three weeks of age, the Canaan will bark in reaction to a stranger approaching, whereas other breeds will usually just whimper for attention, if aware of the stranger at all. By two to three months of age, there is often serious quarrelling among litter-

Bay Path's Jersey Girl Tasha's first snow (CGC, TDI).

mates which can result in the less dominant pups being chased away from their food dish and being completely terrorized by the dominant pups of the litter. Litters as young as this often have to be split up with the pups kept in pairs; we have seen cases of litters "packing" weaker pups, even to the extent of killing them. At this age, the puppies also show very pronounced aggression to "outside" dogs approaching their territory, to the point of attempted attack and hysterical barking.

One interesting factor that we have observed among Canaan pups is the definite difference, from a very early age, between the dominant members of a litter, which we call the "alpha" pups, and the pups with a more submissive temperament. It is possible to identify the alphas by three to four weeks of age. They are dominant, and control their litter-mates. Very frequently, the alpha puppies are also the best looking pup-pies in the litter. If there are several alpha personalities in one litter, they usually have to be separated at an early age or there will be serious fighting.

The second litter born in Holland. Mother is Katzefet, father Tsur me Shaar Hagai.

Above: Typical Canaan puppies of excellent type.

Semel at 6 weeks.

67

Another point we have observed in Canaan pups, and which we consider to be connected in general with their independence of nature and their dislike of being confined, is their aversion to learning to walk on lead. Most Canaan puppies, no matter what age (and we have tried with young puppies of 5 to 6 weeks, up to near adults) when first put on a collar and lead tend to show extreme anxiety, even to the point of panic, resistance and fighting. It is often a question of a number of lessons carried on with great patience before the puppy will accept the necessity of giving in to this restraint and limitation of his freedom.

Keely at the age of 8 weeks.

Keely as an adult. *Photo by Gemma Giannini.*

Raising Canaan puppies

It is very important that the Canaan puppy is raised and handled properly from the beginning. Because of his unique temperament and behavior patterns, it is extremely easy to ruin a puppy through lack of proper attention and to turn him into an overly suspicious, frightened, or overly aggressive adult.

8-week-old Tasha sleeps with favorite toy.

8-week-old Tasha explores her new home.

5-month old Tasha likes to climb sand dunes—even if they are at the Jersey shore.

7-month old Tasha at home.

Tasha at 7 months.

Puppies must be properly socialized; that is, from a very young age they must be handled, petted, and fussed over. Above all, they must be handled with great patience and much encouragement. The Canaan's native characteristics of independence and suspiciousness make him react to things differently from puppies of other breeds. Whereas puppies of most breeds will, in new situations or circumstances, accept change cheerfully and without undue notice, the Canaan, from young puppyhood, will treat every change, new object, new experience, and new person, as a cause for great suspicion. He must be allowed to "look things over," be reassured and encouraged, but should not be forced to react (for instance, to approach a stranger) before he has "made up his mind" about the situation. It should be clear that the Canaan's reaction is not due to fear, but to a very highly developed sense of suspiciousness about anything unfamiliar. This suspiciousness is indeed one of the major reasons that this breed still exists, in the wild as well as in domesticity.

The Canaan puppy should have a great deal of handling, by a variety of people, from a young age; this way he will learn that people are "friends" and will not be overly suspicious of "people" in general. He should, as early as possible and certainly by about three months of age, be taken out and exposed to new places, to traffic, to crowds, to strange surroundings, to riding in cars—to the things that he will be expected to cope with as an adult. A Canaan who has been isolated from experiencing such things as a puppy may be difficult to handle as an adult, and may resist adjusting to new experiences.

Maayan and toy.

Einav me Shaar Hagai at four months. Bred by Shaar Hagai Kennels and owned by Gaby Stoeckle, Diedorf-Biburg. Sire: Tsur me Shaar Hagai; Dam: Tehiyah me Shaar Hagai.

Headstudy of Spatterdash Dreidle. Breeder: Jay Sheaffer; Owner: Bryna Comsky, HaAretz Kennels, Hoffman Estates, Ill. Best In Show, CCA Specialty 1977-1978 and 1979-1980. Sire: Aleph of Star Pine; Dam: Petra of Petach Tikva (Import).

canaans in
north america 7

*(Information for this chapter was kindly provided
by Bertha Sheaffer of Spatterdash Kennels)*

The history of the Canaan Dog in North American started when
the late Mrs. Jack (Ursula) H. Berkowitz brought the first four imports
into California on September 7, 1965. From early February 1964 an ex-
tensive correspondence had been carried on between Ursula and Dr.
Rudolphina Menzel (Ph.D., Assoc. Professor for Animal Psychology, University Tel Aviv) who had been responsible for the rescue of this versatile and distinctive breed from the edge of extinction.

The four Canaan Dogs arrived on the Israeli liner Yehuda after
spending six long weeks on board and traveling over 8,000 miles from
Haifa, Israel to Los Angeles, California. The captain of the Yehuda, a
great dog lover, saw to it that the dogs arrived in excellent condition.

The four Canaan Dogs were Toro me Isfija, IKC 366, a black and
white male bred by the Druse people and purchased from them by Dr.
Menzel for Ursula Berkowitz; Birion me B'nei HaBitachon, IKC 355,
black and white male bred by the Israel Institute for Orientation and
Mobility of the Blind; Waf me Massada, IKC 364, black and white female
bred by Bedouin tribesmen and purchased from them by Dr. Menzel;
Belith me B'nei HaBitachon, IKC 7/356, black and white female bred
at the Israel Institute for the Orientation and Mobility of the Blind.

Ursula Berkowitz had given her solemn promise to Dr. Menzel to
help her establish the breed in America, thereby improving the chances
that this breed that had been redomesticated for only 35 years and was
still in the creative stage, would gain international recognition. With this
goal in mind, Ursula wrote a small pamphlet using extracts from a book
Dr. Menzel had written called "Pariah Hunde," published in 1960. The
pamphlet updated some of the original information, gave descriptions
and pictures of her four imports, and included the breed standard. These
pamphlets were distributed to all interested dog enthusiasts.

The first litter of USA-born Canaan Dog puppies by Birion me Bnei HaBitachon ex Waf me Massada, was whelped on November 24, 1965. From six whelps came one outstanding male, Aleph of Star Pine, CCA 5. The second litter, by Toro me Isfija ex Belith me Bnei HaBitachon, whelped December 31, 1965, also contained six whelps, the most outstanding being Buba of Star Pine, CCA 12.

Mr. Jay C. Sheaffer and his wife Bertha, breeders of fine Dalmations in their Spatterdash Kennels, became interested in the Canaan Dog after seeing a picture and article that appeared in the December 1965 issue of *Popular Dogs Magazine*. The Sheaffers had been looking around for a second breed, and on June 8, 1966, Aleph of Star Pine and Buba of Star Pine were flown east to their new owners who were the first buyers of American-bred Canaan Dogs.

Aleph was from the very first a fine animal; highly intelligent, healthy, willing, and prepotent. Three-fourths of all Canaan dogs registered in the Canaan Club of America Studbook are descendents of Aleph. Buba of Star Pine never came up to the expectation of her proud owners as a brood bitch, never adjusted to her new surroundings and eventually, in spring of 1969, had to be put to sleep.

Aleph of Star Pine (at 10 years of age), the first Canaan Dog born in the U.S. Bred by Ursula Berkowitz. Owned by Jay Sheaffer. Sire of many quality offspring, including multiple breed winners.

Petra me Petach Tikva, 7th import to the U.S. from Prof. Menzel. Owned by Jay Sheaffer, Spatterdash Kennels, Emmaus, PA. Dam of five litters sired by Aleph of Star Pine; one of the foundation bitches of the Canaan Dog in the U.S.

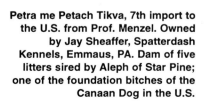

THE CANAAN CLUB OF AMERICA (CCA)

The Canaan Club of America, Inc. (CCA) was formed by Ursula Berkowitz with the arrival of the first four Canaan Dogs from Israel. CCA officers were formally elected in 1969:

President - Mr. David M. Hill, South Bend, Indiana
Vice President - Mr. Jay C. Sheaffer, Emmaus, Pennsylvania
Corresponding Secretary - Mrs. Judith K. Ardine, St. Charles, Michigan
Treasurer - Mrs. Martha Kovitz, Palm Springs, California
Board of Directors - Mrs. Lillian Miller, Seattle, Washington
Mr. Milton Sacks, Flint, Michigan
Mrs. Audrey Bieman, Vero Beach, Florida
Mrs. Barbara Burr, Des Moines, Iowa
Mr. Donald Smith, Madison, Wisconsin
Mr. Alan Goodman, Wilmington, Delaware

By-laws were adopted in March 1971 and the Canaan Club of America Breed Standard was adopted on May 5, 1973. Mrs. Berkowitz did not live to see the Breed Standard adopted for she passed away in 1972.

In the early years of the Canaan Dog in the USA, the club had the pleasure of meeting, on July 19, 1969, Miss Elizabeth Csengeri from Israel. The meeting was at the home of Ursula Berkowitz and served as a breed advisory session and exhibition of Canaan Dogs by their proud owners from the California area. The people in the rest of the country who were unable to attend sent photographs of their dogs to the meeting for a special judging and evaluation.

The first Canaan Club of America Specialty Match, May 28, 1972, at Spatterdash Kennels, Emmaus, PA.

CCA. Ch. Lahatut me Shaar Hagai with owner Victor Kaftal.

Jay Shaeffer set up and controlled the Stud Book from 1968 through 1975. Mrs. Marguerite Lachs served after him for over 15 years. The current Stud Book Guardian is Ms. Bryna Comsky.

Due to the foresight of some of the pioneers of the breed, the genetic pool of today's Canaan Dogs was augmented by the import of a number of Canaans from Israel. These included:

Name	Israeli #	U.S. #	Sex	Importer
Gwira me B'nei HaBitachon	Can.D.385	CCA 33	Female	Mrs. Jack Berkowitz
Dimona me B'nei HaBitachon	Can.D. 391	CCA 34	Female	Mrs. Jack Berkowitz
Petra of Petach Tikva	Can.D. 398	CCA 35	Female	Mrs. Jay C. Sheaffer
Tur me B'nei HaBitachon	Can.D.60/415	CCA 48	Male	Mrs. S. Herwald
Keter me B'nei HaBitachon	Can.D. 68/423	CCA 50	Male	Mrs. David Hill
Kinnereth me B'nei HaBitachon	Can.D.71/46	CCA 51	Female	Sam Prizant
Teva me B'nei HaBitachon	Can.D.63/418	CCA 52	Female	Dr. James S. Elder
Tayara me B'nei HaBitachon	Can.D.65/420	CCA 49	Female	Mrs. Jay C. Sheaffer
Limor me B'nei HaBitachon	Can.D. 96/450	CCA 71	Female	Mrs. Jay C. Sheaffer
Liorah me B'nei HaBitachon	Can.D. 99	CCA 72	Female	Mrs. David Hill
Pat me B'nei HaBitachon	Can.D. 117	CCA 91	Male	Dr. and Mrs. Bruce Kaplan
Nitzah me B'nei HaBitachon	Can.D. 103/457	CCA 92	Female	Dr. and Mrs. Bruce Kaplan
Peera of Petach Tikva	Can.D. 399	CCA 100	Female	Dr. Elmer C. Robnett
Nadav me B'nei HaBitachon	Can.D.100	CCA 101	Male	Dr. Martin L. Norton
Mookie of Talpiot	Can.D. 159	CCA 159	Female	Mr. and Mrs. Bruce Kahn
Hora me Shaar Hagai	Can.D. 187	CCA 140	Female	Mrs. Frances Beard
Atarat HaTeva me Shaar Hagai	ISBR 10936	CCA 259	Female	Mrs. Evelyn Slonim
Kaspit me Shaar Hagai (Canada)	ISBR 23836	CCA 366	Female	Mrs. Suzan Horovitch
Atar of Shaar Hagai	ISBR 29294	CCA 425	Male	Mrs. Frances Beard
Gover of Shaar Hagai (Canada)	ISBR 29299	CCA 426	Male	Florence Hogarth
Arad of Shaar Hagai (Canada)	ISBR 31434	CCA 443	Male	Mrs. Terry Bagley
Romach of Shaar Hagai (Canada)	ISBR 35936		Male	Mrs. Kathleen Wills
Tsabarit of Shaar Hagai	ISBR 36457		Female	Tom Ingram
Tsafra of Shaar Hagai	ISBR 36458		Female	Dr. Bernard O. Nemoitin

Sagiv of Shaar Hagai	ISBR 44419		Male	Gary L. Annis
Segula of Shaar Hagai	ISBR 44420		Female	Gary L. Annis
Yedid of Shaar Hagai	ISBR 47098		Male	Sheldon Howard
Lahatut of Shaar Hagai	ISBR 55523		Male	Victor Kaftal
Maayan of Shaar Hagai	ISBR 55529		Female	Mrs. Ellen Klein
Moses of Shaar Hagai	ISBR 55530		Male	Danny Tsafrir
Ksufa of Shaar Hagai	ISBR 53294		Female	
Nodedet of Shaar Hagai	ISBR 56565		Female	Charles Hockenberry
Karmit Beit Kuti	ISBR 57274		Female	Mrs. Terry Bagley
Gvir of Shaar Hagai	ISBR 60852		Male	Mrs. Ellen Klein
Hila of Shaar Hagai	ISBR 61355		Female	Mrs. Ellen Klein
Holit of Beit Dada	ISBR 62492		Male	Victor Kaftal
Shoham of Shaar Hagai	ISBR 60423		Female	Bryna Comsky

The Canaan Club of America has held twenty-one Annual Specialty Shows from 1972 to 1992. The first show was at Spatterdash Kennels in Emmaus, Pennsylvania, on May 28, 1972. There was a total of 14 entries representing nine states at that first historic competition. The following list details this and subsequent shows:

Date: May 28, 1972
Best Puppy in Show: Ketora's Hadassah bat Keter, Owner: Dr. Aaron Shinebein
Best of Opposite Sex: Ketora's Hadassah bat Keter
Judge: Miss Tess Hensler   Location: Emmaus, PA

Date: Sept. 2, 1973
Best Puppy in Show: Hora me Shaar Hagai, O: Frances Beard
Best of Opposite Sex: Adam me Beth HaEmunah, O: Judith Ardine
Judge: Margaret H. Meminger   Location: Youngstown, OH

Date: June 30, 1974
Best Puppy in Show: Hora me Shaar Hagai, O: Frances Beard
Best of Opposite Sex: Spatterdash Yawvin, O: Marguerite Lachs
Judge: Patricia Speight   Location: North Hollywood, CA

Date: May 25, 1975
Best Puppy in Show: Jo-Lain's Baruch Jacob, O: John Carroll
Best of Opposite Sex: Bsorah bat Canaan, O: Judith Ardine
Best in Show: Bartholomew ben Canaan, O: Judith Ardine
Judge: Florise M. Hogan   Location: Chicago, IL

Date: July 4, 1976
Best Puppy in Show: Von Karstadts Asher, O: Beatrice & Phillip Karstadt
Best of Opposite Sex: Spatterdash Limor, O; Bryna Comsky
Best in Show: Padre's Shekvar von Karstadt, O: Beatrice Karstadt
Judge: Michael A Cianchetti   Location: Philadelphia, PA

Date: August 13, 1977
Best Puppy in Show: Kaspit me Shaar Hagai, O: Susan Horovitch
Best of Opposite Sex: Kaspit me Shaar Hagai
Best in Show: Spatterdash Dreidle, O: Bryna Comsky
Judge: Wayne Fessendon   Location: Oklahoma City, OK

Date: August 12, 1978
Best Puppy in Show: Atar me Shaar Hagai, O: Frances Beard
Best of Opposite Sex: Zipporah of Massada, O: Barbara Burr
Best in Show: Spatterdash Dreidle, O: Bryna Comsky
Judge: J. Ward Allen   Location: Naples, FL

Date: August 12, 1979
Best Puppy in Show: Ha'Aretz Miryam Carrie, O: Bryna Comsky
Best of Opposite Sex: same
Best in Show: Spatterdash Dreidle, O: Bryna Comsky
Judge: Miss Ellener N. Gesler   Location: Alamogordo, NM

Date: August 10, 1980
Best Puppy in Show: Beth Din's Amy, O: Hinda Bergmen
Best of Opposite Sex: Southalta's Beriah, O: Terry Bagley
Best in Show: Spatterdash Dreidle O: Bryna Comsky
Judge: J. Bruce Chappell   Location: Raleigh, NC

Date: August 8, 1981
Best Puppy in Show: Beth Din's Adrian, O: Donna Dodson
Best of Opposite Sex: same
Best in Show: Southalta's Beriah, O: Terry Bagley
Judge: Diane Malenfant   Location: Scottsdale, AZ

Date: June 12-13, 1982
Best Puppy in Show: HaAretz Ayen Aleph J. Maccabee, O: B. Comsky
Best of Opposite Sex: Spatterdash Limor, C.D., O: Barbara Burr
Best in Show: Int. Mex. Ch. Joshua of Grey Mesa, O: Barbara Burr
Judge: Jay C. Sheaffer   Location: DeKalb, IL

Date: June 9-10, 1983
Best Puppy in Show: Beth Din's Beruriah, O: L. Bergman & T. Chafkin
Best of Opposite Sex: Spatterdash Limor, C.D., O: B. Comsky
Best in Show: Int. Mex. Ch. Joshua of Grey Mesa, O: Barbara Burr
Judge: Robert Ligon   Location: Houston, TX

Date: October 14, 1984
Best Puppy in Show: HaAretz Rashe Chavala of Geva, O: L. Stephens
Best of Opposite Sex: Terramara's Beka, O: Terry Bagley & Krista Dinney
Best in Show: Int. Mex. Ch. Joshua of Grey Mesa, O: Barbara Burr
Judge: Wayne Fessondon   Location: Oklahoma City, OK

Date: September 8, 1985
Best Puppy in Show: Ariel Shin Ha'Aretz of Briel, O: Ellen Klein
Best of Opposite Sex: Int. Mex. World CCA CH. Beth Din's Witch's Brew,
   B/O: Hinda Bergman
Best in Show: CCA CH. Ha'Aretz Ayen Aleph J. Maccabee CCA TD,
   O: Bryna Comsky
Judge: Maxwell Riddle   Location: Ravenna, OH

Date: August 10, 1986
Best Puppy in Show: Pleasant Hill Dassi, O: Donna Dodson
Best of Opposite Sex: Gevaht Noam Shelah, O: Donna Dodson
Best in Show: Terramara's Achad, O: Terry Bagley
Judge: Mr. Robert Edison   Location: Alamogordo, NM

Date: July 11-12, 1987
Best Puppy in Show: Terramara's Ezara of Marega, O: Margie Lachs
Judge: Mrs. Jacqueline Brown
Best of Opposite SEx: Terramara's Ezara of Marega, O: Margie Lachs
Best in Show: Ariel Shin Ha'Aretz of Briel, O: Ellen Klein
Judge: Avi Marshak (Israel)   Location: West Winfield, NY

Date: June 5, 1988
Best Puppy in Show: Geva's Jessie of Briel, O: Ellen Klein
Best of Opposite Sex: CCA Ch. Gevaht Noam Shelah, O: Donna Dodson
Best in Show: CCA CH. Ariel Shin Ha'Aretz of Briel, O: Ellen Klein
Judge: Mr. Alfred Treen   Location: Kingston, IL

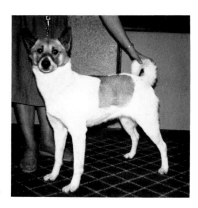

CCA Ch. Geva's Jessie of Briel.

Date: October 1, 1989
Best Puppy in Show: Terramara's Flavian, O: Donna Dodson
Best of Opposite Sex: CCA Ch. Atar of Shaar Hagai, O: Frances Beard
Best in Show: CCA Ch. Donbar's Mona Lisa, O: D. and B. Burr
Judge: Mrs. Nancy Perrell   Location: Scottsdale, AZ

Date: October 11, 1990
Best Puppy in Show: Jomar's Kia of Grey Mesa O: Daniella M. Schooley
Best of Opposite Sex: Beth Din's Amy, O: Gerald and Shirley Pierce
Best in Show: CCA Ch. Ariel Shin Ha'Aretz of Briel O: Ellen Klein
Judge: Clifton Shryock   Location: Alamogordo, NM

Date: July 14, 1991
Best Puppy in Show: Pleasant Hill Sapir O: Donna Dodson
Best of Opposite Sex: CCA Ch. Pleasant Hill Yetta, O: Donna Dodson
Best in Show: CCa Ch. Lahatut me Shaar Hagai CCA CD AKC/CCA
   CDX TT, O: Victor Kaftal
Judge: Dr. Robert J. Berndt   Location: Elmhurst, IL

Date: July 10, 1992
Best of Opposite Sex: Pleasant Hill Yetta, O: Donna Dodson
Best in Show: CCA Ch. Ariel Shin Ha'Aretz of Briel, O: Ellen Klein
Location: Stowe, VT

Many CCA members volunteered time and work to promote the Canaan Dog by participating in exhibitions, parades, county fairs, television programs, and many other promotional activities. They also showed at match and point shows in Mexico (Mexico is a member of the FCI) resulting in a number of Mexican championships.

On June 1, 1989, the Canaan Dog was recognized by the American Kennel Club and entered in the Miscellaneous class. Canaans are now being shown in official AKC point shows all over the country. The next goal of the CCA is to obtain full recognition and group status for the breed. With this goal in mind, the Club is in regular contact with the AKC, and continuing with fresh energy in their promotion of the breed.

Following is a list of titles awarded by the CCA up to 1991. (The list may not be complete.)

Mex., CCA Ch. Toro me Isfija
Mex., CCA Ch. Hora me Shaar Hagai
Mex., CCA Ch. Spatterdash Veda m'Padre
Mex., CCA Ch. Luke of Shalom
CCA Ch. Spatterdash Dreidle CCA TD
Int. Mex. CCA Ch. Joshua of Grey Mesa
Mex. CCA Ch. Chia of Grey Mesa
World, Mex. CCA CH. Southalta's Gabriella
World, Mex. CCA CH. Amos of Grey Mesa
Mex. CCA Ch. Atar me Shaar Hagai
CCA Ch. Massada's Delilah
Mex. CCA CH. Mr. Able of Panda Bear
CCA Ch. Hagunah of Massada

CCA CH. Adam me Beth HaEmunah

CCA Ch. Padre's Yafit von Karstadt

CCA Ch. Spatterdash Limor, CCA CD

Int.Mex.World,Ch of the Americas CCA CH. Beth Dins Witch's Brew

Int.Mex.World,Ch.of the Americas, CCA Ch. Beth Din Sorcerer's Apprentice

Vavi Bat Mookie of Talpiot, CCA CD

CCA Ch. Ha'Aretz Ayen Aleph J. Maccabee, CCA/AKC TD

Int.Mex. CCA Ch. DonBar's Mona Lisa

Ha'Aretz Rashe Chavala of Geva CCA CD

CCA Ch. Terramara's Bithia

Gevaht Noam Marnina Hannah CCA/AKC CD

CCA CH. Terramara's Bekah, CCA CD

CCA Ch. Pleasant Hill Dassi, HC

Int.Mex. CCA Ch. Terramara's Achad

CCA Ch. Beth Din's Adrian

CCA Ch. Jehovah Jireh Jael m'Grey Mesa

Kora of Massada CCA CD

Samach Rebecca Waf Ha'Aretz CCA CDX, HC

CCA CH. Arad me Shaar Hagai

Gevaht Noam Ahuva CCA CDX

CCA CH. Terramara's Dawneeayl Doron, HC

CCA Ch. Briel's Adiv Ben Ariel

CCA CH. Ariel Shin Ha'Aretz of Briel

CCA CH. Gevaht Noam Shelah

Ha'Aretz Mem Dreidleson CCA TD

Geva's Kadesh Kalil Ben Dovev, HC

CCA Ch. Pleasant Hill Yetta

CCA CH. Terramara's Calah

CCA CH,. Geva's Jessie of Briel

CCA Ch. Shvatim Confidence, HC CGC

CCA Ch. Gevaht Noam Dodi

CCA Ch. Pleasant Hill Nili

Int. Ch. of the Americas, Mex. Ch. Jomar's Ginger of Grey Mesa

CCA Ch. Lahatut me Shaar Hagai, AKC UD, UKC CDX

THE ISRAEL CANAAN DOG CLUB OF AMERICA (ICDCA)

In 1994, the Israel Canaan Dog Club of America was established. The purpose of this club was to encourage the breeding of Canaan Dogs that would conform to the international FCI standard. It was felt by the founders that some of the breeding in the US was vying away from the desirable type of Canaan, as established by the parent club in Israel, and that there was a serious danger of the breed being split into "Israeli type" and "American type". Such a variation could seriously endanger the development of a breed that was still considered a rare breed and that was still present, both inside and outside of Israel, in relatively small numbers. The new club felt also that it was important to develop contacts with the various Canaan breed clubs and breeders in other countries, in order to work together with them for the preservation and development of the breed.

The club has attracted many members who are active in promoting the true Israeli type of Canaan. There have been two national specialty shows to date with a third in the planning. The club also publishes a highly informative newsletter, Desert Tracks, and sponsors seminars and other activities for the good of the breed. New members are welcomed.

FOUNDATIONS

This is perhaps the place to mention some of the dedicated breeders and fanciers of the Canaan; without their devotion to the breed and its promotion, the Canaan would not have reached its present recognition.

Spatterdash Kennels, Jay and Bertha Shaeffer

Jay and Bertha Shaeffer were a primary force behind the development of the breed in the U.S. As well as being among the first serious breeders, they devoted a great deal of time and energy to promoting the Canaan in all possible ways, and were active in the Canaan Club of

Spatterdash Yawvin, Breeder: Jay Sheaffer; Owner: M. Lachs. BOS, CCA Specialty, 1974. Sire: Aleph of Star Pine Dam: Limor me Bnei HaBitachon (Import)

Import Mex. Ch. Hora me Shaar Hagai at 8 months of age. Breeder: Shaar Hagai Kennels, Owner: Francis Beard, Alamogordo, N.M. Best of Breed, CCA Specialty, 1974. Sire: Isr. Ch. Laish me Bnei HaBitachon; Dam: Dina me Darom.

Import Arad me Shaar Hagai, bred by Shaar Hagai Kennels and owned by Terry Bagley, Terramara Kennels, Grand Centre, Alta., Canada. Winner of Open Dogs, CCA Specialty, 1983 Sire: Samar me Shaar Hagai, Dam: Isr. Ch. Zaaka me Shaar Hagai.

Padre's Shekvar von Karstadt, breeder: Fr. Elmer C. Robnett, Owner: Beatrice Karstadt. Best in Show, CCA Specialty 1976. Sire: Mex. Ch. Spatterdash Veda m'Padre Dam: Padre's Hagit April.

Southalta's Beriah, bred by Suzan Horovitch, owned by Terry Bagley. BOS at CCA Specialty in 1980 and Best in Show at CCA Specialty in 1981. Sire: Adam me Beth Emunah, Dam: Massada's Eve.

America from its foundation. Although the Sheaffers are now retired, the contribution of their Spatterdash Canaans to the development of the Canaan Dog in the U.S. cannot be forgotten.

Beth Din Canaans, Hinda Bergman

Hinda Bergman first became involved with the Canaan Dog in late 1977 when she acquired Vavi Bat Mookie of Talpiot and Lilah Bat Mookie of Talpiot from Rabbi Bruce Kahn. She attended her first Specialty Match in Naples Florida in 1978 and from then on never missed a specialty until her tragic death from cancer in June 1988. She had a great love for the breed and worked tirelessly towards its acceptance by the AKC. She bred quality dogs, including the 1985 Specialty BOS, Int. Mex. World CCA CH. Beth Din Witch's Brew. She was also very interested in obedience, and had titled dogs to prove it. Her breeding remains as an influence behind some of the winners of today.

Geva Canaan Dogs, William and Lorraine Stephens

The Stephens have been active both as breeders and as club officers for many years. As well as breeding show winners, they have concentrated on good temperaments, and some of their dogs have proven themselves as herding dogs as well.

Ha'Aretz Canaan Dogs, Bryna Comsky

Bryna Comsky started with two dogs from early litters from the Spatterdash Kennels, Spatterdash Dreidle, a dog, and Spatterdash Limor, a bitch. Both were highly successful in the show ring and also as producers and can be found in the pedigrees of many of today's Canaans. Bryna has had a good deal of success in the show ring with dogs of her breeding, and is also the first Canaan owner to achieve a Tracking title. She has been very active in both the national breed club and in the regional Great Lakes Canaan Club, of which she was a founder. She has also translated Prof. Menzel's book, "Pariahunde" from the original German; the translation is available through the CCA.

Pleasant Hill (Gevaht Noam) Kennels, Donna Dodson

Donna's continued success as a breeder can be seen in the list of winners she has produced, including a number of National Specialty winners. She has also achieved obedience titles with some of her dogs. She has been active in both the national and the GLCC.

Briel Kennels, Ellen Klein

Ellen became a true part of the dog fancy in 1977 with the acquisition of her first show dog, a Bernese Mountain Dog, and bred her first litter of Bernese in 1979. She has bred and/or owned nine champions, with two more dogs pointed. Her foundation bitch and two of her off-spring have acquired Top Producer awards from the Bernese Mountain Dog Club of America.

In 1980 she acquired her first Tibetan Spaniel, prior to their full recognition by the AKC. Since their recognition eight years ago, she has owned or bred 19 champions, has had a dog in the top ten in the U.S. for the last three years, and has had three dogs earn ROM, with two more close to this award.

She acquired her first Canaan in 1984 when she purchased an 18 month old bitch, Beth Din's Tabatha Beruriah (called Xena), as a wedding gift for her husband. The next addition was a four month old puppy dog, who became CCA Ch. Ariel Shin Ha'Aretz of Briel, who on July 10, 1992 went BOB at the Canaan Club of America specialty for the fourth time — the fourth specialty he attended as an adult. (He was 7 months old the first time he went to a specialty and was Best Puppy at that one). She bred her first litter in 1985 and Ariel and Xena produced eight puppies, seven of which were males. Four of those are still with Ellen. One pup from that litter, Briel's Adiv Ben Ariel, was Best Puppy in Show his first time out, but sadly was later lost to a rare virus.

Her next litter arrived Dec. 12, 1989 when Ariel and CCA Ch. Geva's Jessie of Briel produced seven puppies. One of those puppies, a bitch, Briel's Geva Shoshanna Shirah, went BOS in Sweepstakes and RWB from the puppy class at her first show, the CCA Silver Jubilee show in New Mexico in Oct. 1990 where her sire went BOB.

Ellen is presently living in England, where she is actively breeding and showing Canaans, and remains a board member of the ICDCA.

CCA Ch. Lahatut me Shaar Hagai
UD—first UD Canaan in the U.S.

CCA Ch. Ha'Aretz Ayen Aleph
J. Maccabee, T.D.

Victor Kaftal

Although Victor does not yet have a kennel and has not yet become a breeder, we feel he deserves mention here for the great positive publicity he has brought to the breed through the achievements of his dog, CCA Ch. Lahatut me Shaar Hagai, UD, TT, UKC CDX. Victor has exhibited "Gil", as he is called by friends, extensively both in conformation (where among his achievements he has been BOB at the CCA National Specialty in 1991 and BOB several times at the GLCC Regional Specialties) and in obedience, where he has achieved a number of titles and in some cases High in Trial. He has also been awarded the Super Utility Award by Front and Finish Magazine.

"Gil" is a full litter brother to Isr. Italian Ch. World Winner 1992 Lahav me Shaar Hagai (Int. Isr.Ned.Ch. WW 85-6-7-9 Sirpad me Shaar Hagai ex Gali me Shaar Hagai), and Italian, Int. Ch. World Winner 92 Lilith me Shaar Hagai.

Victor now has another imported bitch, Holit Beit Dada.

There are many, many more dedicated members and breeders in the CCA, who we hope will keep up their good work in the development and promotion of the breed.

Canaans in Canada

In January 1993, the Canaan Dog received full recognition from the Canadian Kennel Club. This is the result of many years of work of Canadians involved with the breed.

The first Canaans entered Canada on May 16, 1970. Akiba of Brandywood and Yael of Brandywood, whelped March 23, 1970, bred by Mr. Alan Goodman of Delaware, were the offspring of Aleph of Star Pine and Spatterdash Atarah.

Import Kaspit me Shaar Hagai, bred by Shaar Hagai Kennels in Israel and owned by Suzan Horovitch, Barnwell, Alta., Canada. Best of Opposite Sex at the Canaan Club of America Specialty in 1977 from the puppy class. Sire: Roman me Shaar Hagai, Dam: Isr. Ch. Ayn HaArava me Shaar Hagai.

In the fall of 1971, Suzan and Art Horovitch, breeders of Boxers, Samoyeds, and Brittany spaniels at their Southalta Kennels in Barnwell, Alberta, Canada, after seeing the Canaan Dog advertisements, began to correspond with breeders in the U.S. On November 30, 1971, Massada's Eve was sent from California by Mildred Perry to the Horovitchs. In 1972, Eve was flown to Michigan to be bred to Hadar of Massada at the Beth HaEmunah Kennels. On September 8, 1972, the first litter of Canaans were born in Canada at the Southalta Kennels. This litter of five puppies together with the four adults in Canada (the other adult Canaan was Zayn of Massada) were the foundation stock of the Canadian Canaan Club, which was set up with the Horovitch family as the driving force.

On March 15, 1973, the first elected officers were voted in from twenty members. The president was Arthur Horovitch; vice-president, Herman Roehr; secretary and treasurer, Suzan Horovitch; directors, Dwayne Hoard, Kurt Heller, Margery Goldberg, and Florence Hogarth. Suzan Horovitch was appointed Studbook Guardian.

Massada's Eve was bred a second time to Adam me Beth HaEmunah and from this breeding six puppies were whelped on May 6, 1974, and Southalta's "B" litter was named. Eve was tragically killed by a car on July 21, 1975.

After whelping a litter in the U.S., Adina me Jalon was imported by the Southalta Kennels, on December 19, 1975. The four year old Adina had a temperament that was as lovable as her parents, Aleph of Star Pine and import Kinnereth me B'nei HaBitachon. She was bred to Southalta's Byron on September 5, 1976 and went on to whelp four puppies of the "G" litter. One of these whelps, Southalta's Gabriella, owned by Beverly Biren, went on to be one of the two "World Winners" of Canaan Dogs at the World Show in Mexico in the spring of 1978. The other World Winner was Amos of Grey Mesa, sired by Spatterdash Yawvin ex import Hora me Shaar Hagai, owned by Frances Beard of New Mexico.

Owner Terry Bagley (Canada) with Arad of Shaar Hagai and his daughter, Terramara's Czara of Marega, handled by Joan Capaier.

The first direct import from Israel to Canada, Kaspit me Shaar Hagai, arrived at Southalta Kennels on December 18, 1976. She was bred to Int. Mex. Ch. Joshua of Grey Mesa (a litter brother to World Winner Amos of Grey Mesa), owned by Barbara Burr of Arizona and whelped five puppies on September 30, 1977. Previous to becoming a mother, Kaspit was Best Puppy and Best of Opposite Sex at the National Specialty Show in August 1977.

A description of Canaans in Canada would not be complete with mentioning Mrs. Terry Bagley, Terramara Kennels, the most active Canaan breeder in Canada today. Mrs. Bagley has very actively supported the breed both in the show ring and through community activities. Her showing has included trips abroad to Europe to show her dogs at the FCI World Shows in Israel, Germany and Spain.

Terry has the following to say about her connection with the Canaan Dog:

> *The first time I ever heard of the Canaan Dog breed was in the "Basenji" magazine in 1968. It piqued my interest, but I had just acquired my first Basenji pup and I also had a beagle at the time. But I kept the article in case. . . . In 1969 and 1970 there were other articles in "Dogs" and "Dog Fancy" magazines, they were quite lengthy with a few pictures. The one written by the Schaeffers really sparked my interest. In 1971, Suzan Horovitch wrote in "Dogs in Canada" and that did it! I just had to have one! I got in touch with her immediately and went to visit her and met the Canaan Dog at last. In 1972, we and a few other fanciers founded the Canadian Canaan Club. In May 1974, Soutalta's Beriah was born, out of Massada's Eve and Adam me Beth HaEmunah and I took her home at 7 weeks. She was the right choice, she showed well and produced well. Four years later, I imported Shekvar von Karstadt from the Karstadts in New York and my first litter was whelped in September 1978. In July 1979, Arad of Shaar Hagai arrived from Israel. That same summer, I decided to start showing and off I went to the CCA National Specialty held in New Mexico. It was a great success for my first time in the ring and I have not missed a Specialty since. I attend most regional specialties and several Rare Breed shows each year. I have shown my Canaans in 6 different countries so far — Canada, USA, Mexico, Israel, Germany and Spain. In Canada it took over 20 years of persistance and finally the Canadian Kennel Club has recognized the breed effective January 1993. Over the years, I have bred nine litters, have owned 25 Canaans; 18 of them are still with us, 9 have their Canaan Club of America Championship and 2 have an obedience title. The highlight of my career with the Canaan Dogs came during my stay in Israel*

Terramara's Calah CCA Ch. and Best in Show, Rare Breed Show, Chicago, 1989. Bred and owned by Terry Bagley (Canada). Arad of Shaar Hagai ex Terramara's Agamim.

Terramara's Eleenaw Arad me Shaar Hagai ex Terramara's Bethis. Bred and owned by Terry Bagley (Canada).

Terramara's Dabrath CCA Ch. Arad me Shaar Hagai ex Terramara's Bekah. Bred and owned by Terry Bagley (Canada).

Terramara's Flavian Achad me Shaar Hagai ex Terramara's Bekah. Bred and owned by Terry Bagley (Canada).

CCA Ch. Geva's Jessie of Briel (left) and Maayan me Shaar Hagai (right). Owned by Ellen and Harold Klein, Briel Kennels.

Karmit Beit Kuti at two years old. Owned by Terry Bagley (Canada).

in 1987. Myrna gave me the opportunity to see the Canaan in the wild and with the Bedouin when she took me into the Negev desert. In June 1990 I imported another Canaan from Israel, Karmit Beit Kuti. In regards to clubs, I am President of the Canadian Canaan Club, a Director of the Canaan Club of America and of the Great Lakes Canaan Club.

The breed has increased in popularity in America, and finding good homes for the puppies has become a realistic goal. Canaans have been written up in a number of books; today there is hardly a book on the various dog breeds that does not include the Canaan.

In late August 1970, Professor Menzel made a visit to the U.S.A. to visit family. At that time she visited California to see how the breed was developing. After returning to New Jersey, she called Spatterdash Kennels and arranged a visit to see the Canaan Dogs in the East. While on the East Coast, she lectured on the early history of the breed, pointed out distinctions between the types of Canaan and said she was pleased to see such nice Canaans in the U.S. from one coast to the other. It was indeed a memorable occasion for those in attendance to meet this grand lady and profit from her knowledge of the breed. Menzel at that time was a spry, sharp and alert 82 years old.

Now, nearly thirty years after the four original imports traveled the long eight thousand miles from Haifa Israel to Los Angeles, the American breeders are still trying to meet the challenge of breeding and promoting an ever better Canaan Dog, attempting to come closer to the ideal. With the increasing interest of Canaan owners in training and showing their dogs in conformation and in obedience, as well as a developing interest in herding trials, and with the prospect of complete recognition by the AKC in the near future, it is hoped that the Canaan in America will achieve the quality and recognition toward which Menzel aspired.

Mex. Ch. Shalom's Luke. Owner: Mildred Perry. Sire: Birion me Bnei HaBitachon (one of four original imports); Dam: Leora of Massada.

U-CDX Holit Beit Dada (left) and U-UD Ch. Lahatut me Shaar Hagai, UD, CKC-CDX, TT (right).

Head study of Karmit Beit Kuti at two years old—Canada.

canaans abroad 8

England

The first Canaan, a bitch, was brought into England in 1965. She was born in a wild pack in the Syrian desert, stolen as a puppy by the Bedouin, and later brought back to England. Her original owners were unable to manage her, and she was taken over by Mrs. Connie Higgins. Higgins researched the breeds of the Middle East area, and discovered that Shebaba, as the bitch was called, fitted the description of the Canaan. Higgins corresponded with Professor Menzel and obtained her confirmation that Shebaba appeared to be a Canaan. Higgins then imported a male, Tiron me Bnei HaBitachon, from Menzel, and applied to the

Kensik Khameshee top winning Canaan in England. Owned by Marjorie and David Cording and Mary McPhail.

British Kennel Club for acceptance. In early 1970, the British Kennel Club officially recognized the Canaan Dog.

Tiron and Shebaba did have two litters in England, and Mrs. Higgins also exhibited her dogs at shows, but not much interest in the breed developed, perhaps in part because of the difficulty of importing new stock due to the strict quarantine laws.

Zeta Pride with handler Tim West. (Isr. Ch. Anan me Shaar Hagai ex Kensix Sheshee.) Owned by Steve Payne, England.

There was an extended lull in the development of the breed in England until 1986. Ruth Corner Tribe, who had become fascinated by the breed during several years that she spent living in Israel, decided to reintroduce the Canaans to England. Early in 1986 she imported a bitch in whelp from the Shaar Hagai Kennels in Israel. Isr. Ch. Rotem me Shaar Hagai, whelped a litter of eight puppies (six dogs, two bitches) in quarantine. Rotem then was returned to Israel and the puppies remained in England; puppies born in quarantine can be released after two months. (Sire of this litter was Shimshon me Shaar Hagai.) The litter was registered with the prefix Kensix, and three of the dogs from this litter have been successfully shown. Kensix Rishon, owned by Ruth Tribe, was very successful until business pressures meant that Ruth could no longer attend shows. Kensix Schleeshee (Brand), owned by Mary Macphail, although lightly shown, has had his share of success and qualified for Crufts 1993. He is also a registered therapy dog. Kensix Khameshee, owned by Marjorie and David Cording and Mary Macphail, has been the top winning Canaan in England in 1988, '89, '90 and '91. He was BOB at Crufts '91, '92 and '93; in '89 he was Best Variety Male at Crufts, and in '90 was Best of Variety.

In 1986, Ruth brought in a second bitch, Tehiyah me Shaar Hagai, who also whelped in quarantine and then returned to Israel while her puppies remained in England. This litter consisted of one dog and six bitches. Sire of this litter was Isr. Ch. Yitzhar me Shaar Hagai. This litter was registered with the prefix Baaretz. Unfortunately, none of this litter has been shown.

In 1988, an Isr. Ch. dog, Anan me Shaar Hagai, was also imported into England. Unfortunately, he was never shown, but he did sire two litters before his tragic death due to a traffic accident, and several of his offspring have appeared regularly in the show ring.

Several litters have been born in England in the last few years, and in 1992 a new bitch was imported into England, Mika Beit Kuti, also in whelp. Four puppies were born in the quarantine, two dogs and two bitches, sired by Lehitraot me Shaar Hagai. Both Mika and her puppies have remained in England. At the end of 1992, Sivan me Shaar Hagai, a young dog with two CACs in Israel, and two puppy bitches were imported into England.

The Canaan Club of England was founded in May 1992. Although the Canaan in England is still not able to gain CCs, in many shows there are now classes for Canaans, and since the breed club is active and enthusiastic, it is hoped that quite soon the breed will be raised to CC level. Many activities, including lectures and teach-ins are held by the club; a regular bulletin is published. The breed was also featured in a major article in one of the British dog papers, and is becoming better known by the English public.

Tiron me B'nei HaBitachon and Saffra Shebaba, England.

Leviya me Shaar Hagai, owned by Rachel Hinze Althof, Germany.

Germany

Gadlan me B'nei HaBitachon, sent by Menzel to Mrs. Freia Eisner of East Berlin in 1967, was Germany's introduction to the Canaan. He was trained and used as a seeing-eye dog by his owner. Mrs. Eisner imported a bitch, Menorah me Shaar Hagai, in 1977.

In 1976, a white dog, Nez Hasheleg me Shaar Hagai, was imported by Mr. Peter Eckerlin. In 1979 Nez was winner of the title Weltsieger (World Winner) at the World Show in Bern, Switzerland. He also proved to be a very good working dog, and passed some working dog tests in Germany.

Early in 1977, Karmit me Shaar Hagai was imported by Ms. Rachel Hinze Althof and subsequently became the beloved housepet of Hildegard and Gunther Beilfuss of Cologne. Karmit was shown successfully several times, and in September 1980 became the dam of the first Canaan dog litter born in Germany. The litter of two dogs and three bitches was sired by another import, Boneh me Shaar Hagai, an impressive red dog who won the Bundessieger title in 1980, and was Klubsieger, CAC, VDH-Sieger and Best in Show at the first Championship Specialty Show for Canaans in Germany in 1981.

On Nov. 8, 1978, Gevaht Noam Matana, a female whelped August 6, 1978, sired by Spatterdash Dreidle ex Shalom's Malkaw, became the first American-bred Canaan to be flown to West Germany. On April 25, 1980, HaAretz Ner Tamid, a male, was the second American Canaan

Dog flown over. Tamid was sired by Spatterdash Dreidle ex Spatterdash Limor. These two Canaans, both black and white, were imported to Germany by the Hannapel family. In November 1980, Matana whelped the second Canaan Dog litter born in Germany, consisting of one dog and four bitches.

In 1983, several new puppies were imported: Ayal me Shaar Hagai by the Pohnlein family of Munich, Einav me Shaar Hagai by Gabi Kielwein of Uberlingen, and Leviyah me Shaar Hagai by Rachel Hinze Althof of Cologne.

The Canaan Club of German was founded in 1977, due to the great interest and organizational activities of Ms. Rachel Hinze Althof, who became acquainted with the Canaan Dog during a stay in Israel. The club has been very active in promoting the breed through articles in many journals and newspapers, television programs, appearances at dog shows, and the yearly publication of a Canaan Dog calendar. In October of 1981, they organized their first National Championship Specialty show. Attendance was very good — the show attracted nearly all the Canaans and their owners in Germany. The judge was Ms. Myrna Shiboleth of Shaar Hagai Kennels in Israel. Best in Show was Boneh me Shaar Hagai and Best of Opposite Sex was his German born daughter, Awuka Kalba me HaArava.

Over the last few years, interest in the breed has been growing, and a number of new puppies have been imported into Germany, both from Israel and from other European countries such as Holland and Italy. Ms. Marlies Menge, the well known journalist-author, who became interested

Menora me Shaar Hagai and Gadlan me B'nei HaBitachon, in East Germany.

in the breed when Menorah went to live with her shortly before the death of Mrs. Freia Eisner, subsequently imported two puppies, Shira me Shaar Hagai from Israel, and a male puppy from a litter born in Italy. Shira appears with the author on the cover photo of her new book, *Zuruck Nach Babelsberg*. Gunther and Hildegard Beilfuss have an outstanding young male, Sanlan Hadas Ben Dubah, imported from Holland. The appearance of a number of Canaans at the World Dog Show in Dortmund in 1991, where they were presented in the center ring as the national breed of Israel, attracted a good deal of interest and resulted in several puppies being imported from Israel.

Italy

Several Italian breeders became interested in the Canaan Dog after seeing them at shows in various parts of Europe. The first dog, Gev me Shaar Hagai, a son of Yedid me Shaar Hagai ex Lahava me Shaar Hagai, was exported to Gabriel Carlucci in Naples in 1988. Gev was extensively shown, gaining a number of CAC and CACIBs, and also won the title of Europasieger in 1991. Gabriel subsequently imported a bitch, Zeeva

Int. Italian Ch. W.W. 1991 Edom Beit Kuti.

me Shaar Hagai, a daughter of Int. Ch. Shachmat me Shaar Hagai and Isr. Ch. Rotem me Shaar Hagai, and has since had a litter.

In 1989, Isabella Zirri, a breeder and exhibitor of Siberian Huskies, saw the Canaan Int. Ch. Sirpad me Shaar Hagai and his daughter Ktifa me Shaar Hagai at a show in Belgium and fell in love with the breed. She subsequently imported the dog Edom me Beit Kuti, a son of Int. Ch. Shachmat me Shaar Hagai and Lilith Beit Kuti, and Lilith me Shaar Hagai, daughter of Int. Ch. Sirpad me Shaar Hagai and Gali me Shaar Hagai. These two were shown extensively, both becoming Italian and International Champions. Edom became World Winner in 1991 and Lilith World Winner in 1992. Isabella subsequently imported two bitch puppies from Israel, and purchased the World Winner dog and BOB in Valencia, Spain 1992, Isr. Ch. Lahav me Shaar Hagai, full brother to Lilith, and his kennel mate, the bitch Isr. Ch. Tehilla me Shaar Hagai (Ch. Anan me Shaar Hagai ex Ch. Peela me Shaar Hagai). Lahav has to date won 10 CACIBs, as well as numerous other titles.

Isabella has bred several litters, exhibits extensively and has done a great deal to promote the breed in Italy, including writing articles for a number of canine journals. It is hoped that in the near future, a Canaan Club will be organized in Italy. Isabella Zirri can be contacted at Via 4 Novembre 37, Traversetolo (Parma), Italy.

Int. Isr. Italian Ch. W.W. 1992 Europaser Bundessgr. Lahav me Shaar Hagai, now in Italy, shown at the World Show in Valencia, Spain, 1992.

Finland

The first pair of Canaans were sent to Finland in 1986. These were Noded me Shaar Hagai, a red dog sired by Isr. Ch. Anan me Shaar Hagai (later exported to England) and Hila me Shaar Hagai, a bitch sired by Int. Ch. Sirpad me Shaar Hagai. Several litters were born and registered to this pair. The dogs were later transferred to Kirsi Alatalo.

Another pair of puppies were imported to Finland in 1991 by Teuvo Pulkinnen. The dogs were Sagiv me Shaar Hagai (Lochem me Shaar

Hagai ex Yafit me Shaar Hagai), a dog, and Tzvia me Shaar Hagai (Yahav me Shaar Hagai ex Naava Beit Rubin), a bitch.

Mrs. Alatalo has become very interested in the breed and has begun showing Canaans at international and national shows. Her dogs have begun to attract a good deal of attention. She has also bred several litters, and is interested in promoting the breed. Several additional dogs have been imported. A Canaan dog club has been founded in Finland which is very active and already has over 80 members.

Holland

The first Canaan, Rogelit me Shaar Hagai (Shimshon me Shaar Hagai ex Tamar me Shaar Hagai), a black female, arrived in Holland in October 1981. She was imported by Mrs. Violette Sanders. Several other dogs were imported into Holland during 1982-3, including Katzefet me Shaar Hagai, a cream daughter of Shimshon me Shaar Hagai and Isr. Ch. Zaaka me Shaar Hagai, who has been shown extensively. Several litters of puppies have been whelped in Holland, with some of the offspring being exported to Switzerland, Germany, and even Kenya.

Currently, however, there is little activity in the breed.

Ch. Katzefet me Shaar Hagai (left), and Shachaf me Shaar Hagai (right), Canaan's in Holland.

Switzerland

There are currently several Canaans in Switzerland, including an import from Israel, a bitch sired by Int. Ch. Sirpad me Shaar Hagai ex Holit Beit Kuti. In 1994 and 1995, five additional puppies were imported from Israel. Mrs. Rachel Hinze Althof is now living in Switzerland with her bitch Leviyah; she is one of the founders of the breed in Europe and it is expected that she will help to encourage development of the Canaan in Switzerland.

France

Several Canaans have been exported to France, but there has been no great interest as yet. However, following the appearance of three Canaans at an International Show in France in 1992, and the appearance of an article on the breed in a French dog magazine, there have been a number of inquiries, and it is hoped that the breed will begin to develop more rapidly there.

Monaco

In early 1975, Bat Oren me Shaar Hagai was exported to Monaco as the personal pet of Princess Antoinette de Monaco, a noted dog woman and enthusiast of middle-eastern breeds. The bitch was shown on occasion, and appeared in several magazine articles with her well-known owner.

Denmark

In 1975, the red bitch puppy, Semel me Shaar Hagai, was imported into Denmark by Mrs. Jytte Weiss. Semel was shown extensively, becoming a Danish Ch. and gaining a number of CACIBs. She was also awarded the title of World Winner in 1977 and gained friends for the breed all over Europe.

Danish Ch. Semel me Shaar Hagai, bred by Shaar Hagai Kennels, owned by Jytte Weiss, Denmark. W.W. 1977. Sire: Isr. Ch. Laish me B'nei HaBitachon; Dam: Nachson Netta me Shaar Hagai.

Another puppy from a litter whelped in Germany has also been imported into Denmark.

South Africa

The first Canaan arrived in South Africa in 1977, a white female called Perach Bar me Shaar Hagai. As the Kennel Union of South Africa was associated with the British Kennel Club, there were no problems registering the bitch. Her owner, Daniel Drooz, a journalist, exhibited her, and some interest in the breed developed. However, Mr. Drooz was subsequently reassigned to the U.S. and of course took the bitch with him.

In 1981, five Canaans were imported to South Africa by Professor Smit of the University of Pretoria. The imports included Isr. Ch. Dardar me Shaar Hagai and four puppies. An additional three Canaans, an adult dog, an adult bitch, and a puppy dog, were imported from Shaar Hagai by the South African police. Several more dogs were imported by private owners. Interest in the breed is based in part on the Canaan's potential as a working dog that can function well under difficult climatic conditions and in particularly rough terrain.

Isr. Ch. Dardar me Shaar Hagai (Ch. Ophir Beit Elron ex Nachshon Netta me Shaar Hagai). Group and Best in Show winner, now in South Africa.

A number of litters have been whelped and registered in South Africa; however, the dogs are rarely seen at shows, and are not well known. There has been, to date, no attempt to form a breed club.

Israel

Of course, no description of the Canaan today is complete without information about the breed in Israel. In the early days of the establishment of the breed, both when Prof. Menzel was working to develop a basis for breeding, and in the early days of Shaar Hagai Kennels, the Canaan was not highly valued by the general public in Israel. Accustomed to seeing such dogs with the Bedouin and village Arabs, and wandering free on the outskirts of settlements and in the desert, only those Israelis who had personal experience with the unique characteristics of the breed appreciated the dogs.

Today, however, the Canaan is gaining more and more popularity as a home and family dog, a guard and security dog, and as a protector of herds. There is an ever increasing demand in Israel for a family dog that can adjust comfortably to apartment and city living with limited space and exercise, that is easy to care for, economical to keep, and that will serve the increasingly important function of a guard dog without being overly aggressive or dangerous to children and family friends. More and more Israelis are finding that the ideal dog to fit that description is the Canaan. The Canaan is also greatly in demand by families living in settlements in isolated or dangerous locations.

As, unfortunately, the need in Israel for dogs to guard factories, military installations, and such, increases, with extreme alertness a primary requirement, the Canaan is again being sought out. His alertness to suspicious objects and to strangers makes him very valuable in these times of disguised explosives. More Israelis keeping herds of cattle

Smadar me Shaar Hagai (Zakief me Verushalayim ex Nurit me Bnei HaBitachon), an excellent bitch and an extremely influential producer. Almost all the Shaar Hagai Canaans trace back to her.

and flocks of sheep in pasture conditions are also finding the Canaan indispensible. Dogs are kept with the herds to protect them from wolves, jackals and foxes that are prevalent in range areas. Many of these people have tried other breeds and have returned to the Canaan as the most efficient and effective herd guard dog. The Bedouins, of course, have known this for thousands of years and still use the Canaan for this purpose.

In Israel, the Canaan is a part of the Israel Spitz Dog Club, one of the largest and most active dog clubs in the country. The Canaans are usually well represented at shows and activities of the club. There are an average of 50 puppies registered with the Israel Kennel Club each year. Litters are often booked even before the puppies are born. In 1991, there were 17 litters registered in the Israel Stud Book and in 1992 there were 15 litters, putting the Canaan well up in the top twenty breeds in Israel.

The Canaan has also appeared frequently in the media — newspapers, magazines, and on television. The wins of the Canaans at International and World shows at home and abroad has brought a great deal of pride to the Israeli public.

Following is a list of some of the Canaans that have been most influential in the development of the breed in Israel:

Isr. Ch. Laish me B'nei HaBitachon
"Simi" as he was called, was one of the last and most successful dogs bred by Professor Menzel. A perfectly typical Canaan in all ways, he was purchased by Shaar Hagai Kennels and became the first Israel Champion in the breed. Simi was used extensively at stud and was very influential in the development of the breed.

Some of his best known offspring were:
Isr. Ch. Ophir Beit Elron
Isr. Ch. Orna Beit Elron
Isr. Ch. Ayn HaArava me Shaar Hagai

Isr. Ch. Lapid me Shaar Hagai
A grandson of Laish through his dam, Tamar me Shaar Hagai, Lapid was also a very successful show and working dog and a very influential sire. Some of his better known offspring are:
Isr. Ch. Hama me Shaar Hagai (4 x CACIB)
Isr. Ch. Rotem me Shaar Hagai
Isr. Ch. World Winner 85, Europasieger Raanana me Shaar Hagai
(These three are all daughters of the outstanding bitch Isr. Ch. Zaaka me Shaar Hagai, who also was the mother of Dutch Ch. Katzefet me Shaar Hagai.)

Isr. Ch. Lapid me Shaar
Hagai at three years of age.

Int. Ch. Sirpad me Shaar Hagai with
his son Int. Ch. Shachmat me Shaar
Hagai.

Int. Isr. W.W. 1985-1987 and 1989,
Ned. Ch. Europasgr., Bundessgr., etc.
Sirpad me Shaar Hagai.

Lahava me Shaar Hagai

Lapid's full litter sister, Lahava, though not so successful in the show ring, was also a good producer, and the dam of Isr. Ch. Peela me Shaar Hagai, a bitch (sired by Shimshon me Shaar Hagai, also a very influential stud). Peela's daughter, Isr. Ch. Tehila me Shaar Hagai, now in Italy, is the dam of Isr. Ch. Tadmit me Shaar Hagai, and near Ch. Sivan me Shaar Hagai, now in England.

Lahava was also the dam of Isr. Ch. Yitzhar me Shaar Hagai (sire of one of the foundation litters in England), five times CACIB and Bundessieger Austria, and his litter brothers:

105

Yam me Shaar Hagai
Yahav me Shaar Hagai
Both were very influential stud dogs.

Isr. Ch. Dardar me Shaar Hagai
Now in South Africa, Dardar, though used limitedly at stud, sired Isr. Ch. Zaaka me Shaar Hagai, an extremely successful show and working bitch and an outstanding producer.

Sirpad me Shaar Hagai
Int. Isr. Ned. Ch. World Winner 85-6-7-9, Bundessieger, Europasieger, AmsterdamWinner, Copenhagen Winner, Frankfurtsieger Sirpad me Shaar Hagai is, to date, the breed's top winner and most influential sire. Sirpad is a son of Shimshon me Shaar Hagai and Isr. Ch. Ayn HaArava me Shaar Hagai (a daughter of Laish). He has been a group winner several times, club show BOB, and reserve Best In Show at an Int. all breed show. He is considered by many judges who have seen him to be a perfect example of the breed.

Sirpad has produced many outstanding offspring, some of the best known are:
Isr. Ch. World Winner 1991 Ofra me Shaar Hagai
World Winner 1989 Ktifa me Shaar Hagai
Isr. Int. Ch. Shachmat me Shaar Hagai
Isr. Italian Int. World Winner 1992 Lahav me Shaar Hagai CCA
    CH. Lahatut me Shaar Hagai UD
Italian Int. Ch. World Winner 1992 Lilith me Shaar Hagai
Shira me Shaar Hagai (in Germany) CAC and CACIB winner.

Int. Isr. Ch. Shachmat me Shaar Hagai and Int. Isr. It. Ch. Lahav me Shaar Hagai.

Isr. Int. Ch. WW Shachmat me Shaar Hagai
A son of Sirpad, Shachmat has also proven to be an influential sire. At seven years of age, he has sired many winners, including:

Int. Italian Ch. Edom Beit Kuti
near Isr. Ch. Sivan me Shaar Hagai (now in England)
Isr. Ch. Malka me Shaar Hagai
Karmit Beit Kuti (in Canada)
Isr. Ch., WW Lehitraot me Shaar Hagai – World Winner, Bern 1995
Maayan me Shaar Hagai (in the U.S.)
Gvir me Shaar Hagai (in the U.S.)

Following is a list of Canaans who have become Israel Champions since the recognition of the breed:

Laish me B'nei HaBitachon (Dugma me B'nei HaBitachon ex Lady)

Ophir Beit Elron (Laish me B'nei HaBitachon ex Yekutiella me Yerushalayim)

Orna Beit Elron (Laish me B'nei HaBitachon ex Yekutiella me Yerushalayim)

Dardar me Shaar Hagai (Ophir Beit Elron ex Nachshon Netta me Shaar Hagai) Exported to S.A.

Ayn HaArava me Shaar Hagai (Laish me B'nei HaBitachon ex Smadar me Shaar Hagai)

Zaaka me Shaar Hagai (Dardar me Shaar Hagai ex Petra HaMuv-cheret me Shaar Hagai)

Lapid me Shaar Hagai (Guri me Beit Hakerem ex Tamar me Shaar Hagai)

Hama me Shaar Hagai (Lapid me Shaar Hagai ex Zaaka me Shaar Hagai)

Rotem me Shaar Hagai (Lapid me Shaar Hagai ex Zaaka me Shaar Hagai)

Isr. Ch. Hama me Shaar Hagai.

Raanana me Shaar Hagai (Lapid me Shaar Hagai ex Zaaka me Shaar Hagai)

Sirpad me Shaar Hagai (Shimshon me Shaar Hagai ex Ayn HaArava me Shaar Hagai)

Yitzhar me Shaar Hagai (Noded me Arad ex Lahava me Shaar Hagai)

Peela me Shaar Hagai (Shimshon me Shaar Hagai ex Lahava me Shaar Hagai)

Anan me Shaar Hagai (Tsur me Shaar Hagai ex Tehiya me Shaar Hagai) Exported to England

Tehilla me Shaar Hagai (Anan me Shaar Hagai ex Peela me Shaar Hagai) Exported to Italy

Shachmat me Shaar Hagai (Sirpad me Shaar Hagai ex Tehiya me Shaar Hagai)

Ofra me Shaar Hagai (Sirpad me Shaar Hagai ex Hama me Shaar Hagai)

Malkah me Shaar Hagai (Shachmat me Shaar Hagai ex Mikah Beit Kuti)

Tadmit me Shaar Hagai (Lahit me Shaar Hagai ex Tehilla me Shaar Hagai)

Lahav me Shaar Hagai (Sirpad me Shaar Hagai ex Gali me Shaar Hagai) Exported to Italy

Bat me Shaar Hagai (Lahav me Shaar Hagai ex Mikah Beit Kuti)

Lehitraot me Shaar Hagai (Shachmat me Shaar Hagai ex Reut me Shaar Hagai)

Gur me Shaar Hagai (Sivan me Shaar Hagai ex Tavit me Shaar Hagai)

Isr. Ch. Peela me Shaar Hagai.

Ofri me Shaar Hagai (Roman me Shaar Hagai ex Ch. Ayn HaArava me Shaar Hagai), a near champion, was CAC at Tel Aviv Int. Show in 1983.

Winners of Two CAC to date:

Inbar me Shaar Hagai (Sirpad me Shaar Hagai ex Hama me Shaar Hagai)
Sivan me Shaar Hagai (Shachmat me Shaar Hagai ex Tehilla me Shaar Hagai) Exported to England

Selected References

Clubs:

American Kennel Club
51 Madison Avenue
New York, NY 10010
Call 212-696-8200 to get a number for local breeders

Canaan Club of America
Lorraine Stephens
Box 555
Newcastle, OK 73065

Canaan Dog Club of England
Mrs. Ellen Minto
113 Cranleigh Rd.
Feltham, Middx., TW13 4QA England

Canaan Dog Club of Finland
Kirsi Alatalo
Angervontie 1 A
04260 Kerava, Finland

Canaan Club of Germany
Mrs. Hildegard Beilfuss
Falkenburgstrasse 14
D-5000 Koln, Germany

Israel Canaan Dog Club of America
Dana Pittman
1510 Bailey Morrison Drive
Somerville, TN 38068 USA

Books:

The Complete Dog Book
Official Publication of the AKC
Published by Howell Book House, New York, NY

The Uncommon Dog Breeds
Kathryn Braund
Available from Alpine Publications, Loveland, CO

The Rare Breed Handbook
Dee Gannon
Golden Boy Press, Hawthorne, NJ

A Celebration of Rare Breeds
Cathy J. Flamholtz
OTR Publications, Ft. Payne, AL